The International Politics
of an Embodied God

The International Politics of an Embodied God

Nationalism in Judaism, Christianity and Islam

Stephen Chan, OBE
SOAS University of London

ROWMAN & LITTLEFIELD
Lanham • Boulder • New York • London

Executive Acquisitions Editor: Michael Kerns
Assistant Editor: Elizabeth Von Buhr
Sales and Marketing Inquiries: textbooks@rowman.com

Published by Rowman & Littlefield
An imprint of The Rowman & Littlefield Publishing Group, Inc.
4501 Forbes Boulevard, Suite 200, Lanham, Maryland 20706
www.rowman.com

86-90 Paul Street, London EC2A 4NE

British Library Cataloguing in Publication Information Available

Library of Congress Cataloging-in-Publication Data

Names: Chan, Stephen, 1949- author.
Title: The international politics of an embodied God : Nationalism in Judaism,
    Christianity, and Islam / Stephen Chan, SOAS University of London.
Description: Lanham : Rowman & Littlefield, [2025] | Includes bibliographical
    references and index.
Identifiers: LCCN 2024030201 (print) | LCCN 2024030202 (ebook) |
    ISBN 9798881801403 (cloth) | ISBN 9798881801410 (paperback) |
    ISBN 9798881801427 (epub)
Subjects: LCSH: Nationalism—Religious aspects. | World politics—Religious aspects. |
    Religion and politics.
Classification: LCC BL65.N3 C36 2025 (print) | LCC BL65.N3 (ebook) |
    DDC 201/.72—dc23/eng20240805
LC record available at https://lccn.loc.gov/2024030201
LC ebook record available at https://lccn.loc.gov/2024030202

Contents

Preface

A Meditation on the Book of Job

The Book of Job is in some ways the most evocative of the Old Testament books, but also the most problematic. It has no historical account to render, such as the exodus from Egypt, the sagas of the judges and kings of Israel, the return from captivity to rebuild the temple. It is purely a moral and philosophical debate composed in three parts, probably all written at different times, and utilising a Hebrew that is at once archaic and formal on the one hand – almost like looking back to an ancient form of the language but written by someone for whom it was a second language – and borrowing from Aramaic on the other – that is, from the time of Alexander's influence on the culture of the Middle East. It borrows from regional legends of a just man, famed for his integrity despite all difficulties – and yet his integrity is on behalf of nobody but himself before God. He is not fighting for anyone else. And it is God who, despite any provocation or sin from Job, agrees to test him and have him afflicted by huge losses. Job's family is wiped out as if his sons and daughters were dust to be swept to the wind. Finally, after much learned debate as to the nature of God, sin, and creation, God declares Himself in an almost pettily triumphant way.[1]

Because it intersects with so much other regional legends it reveals a form of inter-discursivity which in fact is a characteristic of the entire Old Testament. But what it introduces as a problem for today's Christianity is something Persian, and that is the equal terms by which God and the Satan figure address each other.

For this Satan is ranked among the 'Sons of God' and is free to come and go from heaven to earth and back again. He appears in the same council of angels as all the others and speaks directly with God – so that he is not only an equal with the other angels but he also assumes an equality at least of rights to debate and bargain with God. Although named 'Satan', he is not necessarily the Satan of later Christian times but, rather, a heavenly creature of dissidence all the same. In some non-biblical accounts, the later Satan comes in particularly radiant form. Satan is a creature of beauty. Reading backwards to the Book of Job it is almost as if, at the end, God's self-declaration as the creator of the Behemoth and Leviathan is an *ex post facto* statement of 'See? I'm really greater than you after all'. God claims to have created these mighty monsters, but he does not claim to have created the dissident Satan. In the early Persian motifs of the elements of the universe, those that led to Zoroastrianism and which, in turn, had a powerful influence on Christianity, light and darkness are equal parts of a cosmic struggle. Light seems to win, but the challenge of nightfall never disappears. The universe, thus, becomes one of equivalence – just as in Job there is equivalence in debate at least between God and the Satan figure.

The problem with the Book of Job is that it is God who is 'sinful', who is happily eager to lay bets on human lives and welfare. Job might have in the end been recompensed with even more riches and children – the number of children meaning his poor wife had to give birth twenty times – but that obscures the fact that human senses of self, of self-value, of full subjectivity and agency, of intelligence and dreams, seven sons and three daughters – were wiped out for a bet.

The accompanying problem is that God not only debates with this Satan on equal terms but He also personally declares to Job's three friends that they were advising Job incorrectly and specifies ritual apologies by way of animal sacrifices and warns He will destroy them unless Job prays for them. Job does so, but before that, God, of course, also speaks to Job. The self-revelation as the creator of monsters like the Behemoth and Leviathan comes to Job directly and personally. In all his boasting of his prowess, God speaks only of things He has created on earth. Dawn and evening – with extra-terrestrial causes in the sun and moon – are mentioned only insofar as earth has a dawn and evening, not that God created the sun and moon and the cosmos. It is a speech concentrated on a petty speck in the universe. In the wider universe, the dissident Satan may not have created anything – as far as we know from God – but he can still saunter in and out of God's court and challenge Him.

As for the Behemoth and Leviathan, these are usually seen as an elephant and a whale, but this Behemoth eats flesh as well as grass, and the Leviathan has a neck and scales and breathes fire – he seems a dragon – and both creatures become comic book monsters like King Kong and Godzilla. There is something finally alarmingly small scale about this God.

That is to seem sacrilegious, since the entire middle portion of the Book of Job is a debate as to the power and, above all, the nature of the justice of God. Finally, however, God declares He is just because He is powerful enough to be just and no one can declare Him otherwise.

The nature of not being able to question the justice of someone supernaturally powerful, of someone who accepts debate only from heavenly creatures but not from humans, renders the position of humans as obedient worshippers – blessed (or not, and not blessed because of whimsy) – without agency but required to have faith in God, in God's justice and in God's final greater greatness than the greatness of anyone else.

God has a full range of human emotions to do with assertiveness, jealousy and spite. He poses a huge range of problems in the study and appreciation of religions of any faith – for these emotions intrude on even the most self-declared serenities of belief and spiritual practice. And the organisation of humans into communities – seeking this kind of God on their side – poses, even more now than in the days of antiquity, special problems for how we perceive and practise choice in the world.

God's chosen people – from the nation of Israel chosen by God for redemption from Egypt, to the passage in the Qur'an in which God declares, 'I have chosen you as a people most just', to God blessing America, God saving the queen, defending New Zealand and saving Africa (in the Xhosa, Zulu and Sesotho portions of *Nkosi sikekel'i Afrika*, but not in the Afrikaans and English verses) – there is around the world a nationalist appropriation of God – protected by, and projecting his power, and vindicated by his justice, while smiting others who, while claiming God is on their side, are clearly less faithful to Him (while manifestly also being less powerful).

The state project, even in modern times from the seventeenth century onwards, has not excused God from the process of national identity and state-building. Zambia is, for instance, despite missionary influence being part of the colonial project, constitutionally a Christian nation. Others are constitutionally Islamic. Institutionalised Buddhism plays a huge role in the ethnic pogroms launched by the states of Myanmar and Sri Lanka. Hindutva legitimates communal persecution in India. China opposes Buddhism under the leadership of the Dalai Lama in Tibet, because he is seen as organising a nation opposed to Chinese state sovereignty over Tibet and as opposing Islam among the Uighurs as an organising force for an alternative nationalism to that of the Han identity and the Chinese state.

Even those who sought an alternative to previously formed religion used symbols and rituals that were essentially religious. Masonic emblems appear on the US currency. The Masonic Lodges were safe havens, confidential societies, where plots against the British could be hatched. The English Revolution of the seventeenth century, while denying the divine right of kings, nevertheless declared that God had made every man (not yet every woman) equal as a foundation for what became the parliamentary state. Faith in God (or opposition to God) became hallmarks of nationalism, credos and emblems of statecraft, and in one's self-declaration as a national identity. Even the 'alternative' English national anthem bruted by anti-monarchists and egalitarianists, Blake's poem, asks whether Jesus once set foot in England's green and pleasant land and, in the name of justice, asks how the 'dark Satanic mills' of industrialisation could be encamped upon the English shores.

Even so, from Milton's great poem, *Paradise Lost*, set against the parliamentary struggle against the king, it is Satan who roused his defeated angels with a heroism that insisted that even God had to prove he was truly just and not just a powerful tyrant. The tension in Job's account of the courts of heaven is here given a role in the contestation for the state.

Notwithstanding the anti-heroism and essentially philosophical justification of rebellion in Milton's poem, most views of one's God are parochial. The medieval crusaders carried a banner of Christ into battle and the enemy were heathens. The Spanish conquistadores massacred the Aztecs, despite their high civilisation and hospitality because of greed for gold, certainly, but fortified in their piracy and ransacking by the assurance that it was they who were Christian and thereby protected in their depredations against those who were not Brethren in Christ. The Afrikaner settlers in South Africa believed the black race was accursed because descended from Ham, Noah's son who laughed at the drunken patriarch after the flood, even though there is no scriptural account that Ham was black or produced a progeny that was black. But God is in one's own image and no one among the settlers dared suggest God might have been black. In Ethiopia, the most ancient Christian state, he most assuredly was.

God becomes, in the broadcast, defence or creation of the state – 'one of our own' – and the state is one of his own, complete with vindictiveness and pettiness. And it is the state that is defended, not a faith in the first instance. The faith, or a specific variation of it, defends the state.

In 1303, when the Mongol invasions spread into the Middle East and they were at the gates of Damascus, Ibn Taymiyyah was one of those sent by the Damascenes to negotiate (in the end, unsuccessfully) with the Mongols. Taymiyyah subsequently became an underground fighter and, later, participated in the great battles that helped drive the Mongols away. He is of interest because he is regarded as one of the great ideologues of jihadism today, a militant defender of the faith – even though he was in many ways more nuanced (and regarded as highly controversial in his day) than his modern followers might suspect.[2] But the point here is that Taymiyyah was defending Damascus. The Mongols, too, were Islamic – although not in the same way as the Damascenes; they did not obey sharia law, for instance, preferring their own legal codes, but all the same regarded themselves as believers. Variations in the same faith can of course be decisive, as the Catholic/Protestant wars in Europe indicate; but those very wars were also wars of nationalism.

In the case of Damascus, a view of national and ethnic identity absorbed its own variation of faith to its cause.

Amidst these contradictions and seeming diminutions of an essential God, this book sets out, in a series of chapters, to discuss the national, ethnic or other proprietary ownership of God. God or the gods are imbued with very human characteristics. They are reduced to the scale of this planet. They have thrones like human kings. In a way it is reminiscent of Homer's tales of Troy, where the gods of Olympus took sides in the great war between the Greeks and Trojans, and were given to spite, favouritism, special pleadings and vindictiveness. The ancient Greek legends are replete with gods raping humans, men and women, cuckolding one another, having beauty contests (judged by a man) and fighting alongside human armies. It is Apollo who personally defeats Patroclus; Hector merely adds the finishing thrust. The gods appear as glamorous but also simply more powerful humans, and Olympus is a courtly society not unlike human social organisation.

God is limited by the human imagination. In a way, the Book of Job was an invitation to expand one's imagination of God. He is greater than humans because humans cannot create the Behemoth and Leviathan. But the imagination does not extend beyond an immediate time and space. And the Behemoth and Leviathan, whom humans are asked to imagine as powerful and complex creations, have no purpose ascribed to them. The appreciation and appropriation of God to sanctify and legitimise state formation and national identity is, by contrast, purposeful. The God of the United States is not Chinese. He is confined to an archetype that conforms to a dominant population and conforms alarmingly to its habits. He doesn't lead people away from sin anymore but blesses their grossest acquisition of money and material blessings. Yet he remains the creator of Leviathan and being thus powerful awards the worshipping nation the patina and practice of his power.

This present book cannot cover everything mentioned above. It delves into the history, practices and rituals – scriptures and ideologies – of godly national power. The first part covers Islam, Judaism and Christianity, what I am calling the 'religions of the Book'. This book, not to be confused with 'the Book', does not seek to impose a theological methodology. Its starting point is that, while there are clear commonalities, each case is sufficiently unique to make unifying conceptual work hazardous. It may provide insights for others to attempt such a project.

Similarly, since religious data is not ascertainable in uniform fashions, this book is not social-scientific but, rather, is a series of meditations familiar with the foundational scriptural texts of each of its case examples. As meditations, it is not even fully 'scholarly' in that very few people can claim equal deep knowledge, and knowledge of discourse, on each of the great religions. I certainly cannot and would not. It may be read as a series of provocations not only to scholars of individual faiths but to national leaders that their underpinnings in faith are constructions and sometimes fraudulent.

Here, the image of the Leviathan may be appropriated out of the context of the Book of Job and used in the way enunciated by Thomas Hobbes. The Leviathan agglomerates what became known as the citizen body into itself as the modern state but uses an ancient technique of the ultimate external validation. The Leviathan has faith in its external validation. If there is one hypothesis that runs through this book, it is that as the power of the Leviathan increases, both externally and internally, the universal magnitude of God decreases. He is made, finally, into a reductionist usage of the state. Finally, the Leviathan of the state tames the Behemoth that was God. But God, through his long legacy of scriptural enunciations, validated by previous states and incarnations of the state, makes it complex. He puts up a hell of a fight. In some cases, as we see in today's international relations, the compromises and accommodation between God and state give rise to powerful problems in the global state system.

So, the 'embodiment of God' is the incorporation of God into the state's regard of itself. God provides validation of the state but also achieves His modern form by association with the state.

Particularly in Christianity, God may also be embodied in human form – God may come down to earth as Jesus. Judaism's expectation of an eventual Messiah looks also to such an embodiment. This outlook certainly does not exist in Islam. It would be a sacrilege to propose what would be a reduction and limitation of the scope of God – who all the same speaks in a human language referencing the condition of the world. The Islamic God is not embodied in human form but, in today's international relations of competitive nationalisms, is embodied by the state – differently so by the states of the Sunni world and that of the Shi'a world. But the Saudi boast that it hosts the holy places, such as Mecca, is a claim to being the earthly kingdom of God.

Because today's international relations are competitive, the second part of this book provides three studies of the uses of religion to crush or dominate those of different religions or, in the case of different conceptions of what a moral nationalism should be, even those in the same country who profess the same religion – but clearly in an incorrect form.

Even the 'gentle' religion of Buddhism can provide a religious foundation for war and slaughter. So, the second part of this book provides some problematisations. If an embodied God, who owns the body?

This book had its genesis in my year-long lecture course at the School of Oriental and African Studies (SOAS), University of London: Religion and World Politics – although the arguments in the course have been greatly elaborated in this book. There was an annual lecture size of about seventy students and auditors, something unusual in a small university like SOAS. What was, however, quite usual was the diversity in my audience. The students were drawn from all over the world, and my introductory lecture always contained the words: 'Please don't be offended by what I say – many of you will subscribe to the faiths I will interrogate – be patient, each of you will be offended in turn'. The students were indeed always patient, and I owe them all a debt as they kindly helped me refine my ideas. My SOAS colleagues, Dr Alexej Ulbricht, in particular, and Professor Arshin Adib-Moghaddam, were always gracious and patient to the point of forbearance. Dr Ulbricht helped me teach and gave purpose to my digressions. The class seems to have produced more students later accepted for graduate studies at Sciences Po in Paris than any other, so we did something right. Many of the students were Islamic and some even reformed jihadists. All were prepared to enter discourse and debate. If there is any hope for a more humane and human view of the Behemoth and Leviathan, it lies with the thoughtful of this generation.

Stephen Chan
Pimlico 2023

Chapter 1

The Religions of the Book
The Embodied God and Judaism

Just as the ancient Greeks had alarmingly 'human' gods, being themselves a form of flesh able to be wounded and enjoy carnal pleasures, and able to be shape-changers precisely to secure carnal pleasures (Zeus as a bull, a swan, an eagle and even a cascade of golden rain), so the religions of what we call the Middle East were populated by spiritual creatures who interacted with humanity. The most potent example is, of course, Jesus Christ, who became human for thirty-three years. But both before and after Jesus, the angels of God interacted with humanity in a form directly analogous with the actions of the Greek gods.

The biblical account leaves out names, but Jewish legends have precise names and identities for those angels who helped cause God's wrath and the flood of Noah. They did so by adding to the carnality that offended God, by forsaking heaven because they fell in love with beautiful women. Azael and Shemhazai began a movement to earth among the angels and the results were offspring that the Bible calls *Nephilim*, a hybrid race with supernatural strength.[1] These were destroyed in the biblical flood. But Azael and Shemhazai, according to the legends, had already joined the legions of Satan, or Sammael, as he was then known, who had rebelled against God. He sought a throne even higher than God's. Part of his dissent was built against the creation of humanity who might secure greater favour from God than the angels themselves. Certainly, Azael and Shemhazai recognised the attractions of humanity, barely distanced from heaven and with similar attributes to those of the angels. But the envy and the rivalry led to war in heaven. In Milton's account, the defeated angels – the fallen angels – regroup in hell and organise defiance. In the legends, it is unclear whether they were, in fact, totally exiled from heaven; hence Satan's wandering back and forth between heaven and

1

earth in the Book of Job[2] – and hence the establishment of a Persian-style equivalence, a stasis between light and dark.

Insofar as much of what we take to be the biblical account of history was in fact composed after the release from captivity in Babylon in 539 BC, as a new nationalist project for the re-founded nation of Israel under the direction of Ezra and his priests, the influences of Babylonian exile and of the Persians who overthrew Babylon were unavoidable. Persian influences were especially attractive because of their disdain for idols, preferring a vision of heavenly forces not able to be materially rendered. But, even before liberation from captivity, well before any Israelite kingdom and its conquest by Babylon, the loosely organised tribes of Israel, a wandering series of herdsmen, encountered influences from throughout the region. Many of the legends and myths that were formed had to be incorporated into Ezra's officialised public history as a mark of authenticity – but that did not set mythologies into stone. At a time of very limited literacy, oral accounts and their fluctuations as they are transmitted from place to place and generation to generation mean a pluralism of inputs and stories emerge.[3] The land of Israel was precisely a crossroads in geographical terms. Apart from Sumerian, later Babylonian and Persian influences, there were certainly those from Egypt – sufficient for both Freud and Edward Said (the latter perhaps cheekily) to ask whether Moses was in fact Egyptian.[4] Greek and even Indian influences can be traced, or at least suggested, in the striking similarities of legends.

The tempting qualities of Eve that led Adam into sin, with a twist on the shape of the serpent, are reminiscent of Indian legend:

> When the Creator had made up His mind to fashion woman, He suddenly noticed that the matter at His disposal had already been entirely used up in the creation of Adam. What did He do? He took the undulations of the serpent, the clinging faculty of the creepers, the trembling of the blade of grass, the erect stature of the reed, the velvet of the flower, the lightness of the leaf, the look of the gazelle, the cheerfulness of the sun-ray, the tears of the cloud, the inconstancy of the wind, the softness of down, the sweetness of honey, the cruelty of the tiger, the burning heat of fire, the freezing effect of ice, and the chattering of the magpie, mixed all these elements together and created woman.[5]

The Haggadah, a ceremonial repository of Jewish myths and legends, has clear Greek influences, and the stories of the death of Joseph, apart from the brief note in the Bible, resemble the Egyptian myths of Osiris. Since, even in the Bible, Joseph became the prime minister of Egypt, this should not be surprising.

Of course, the most noted borrowing into both the Bible and Jewish legend is the story of the flood. The Sumerian account predates the Old Testament/ Hebrew Bible account and its early books, known to Judaism as the Torah.

It was probably absorbed by the Israelites during their Babylonian captivity and officialised into national history upon liberation by the Persians. It was an attractive incorporation as it spoke of a chosen people, cared for by God, who delivered them from destruction. Ezra's new nationalism had to include a history of godly salvation and care, of godly choice. The Old Testament account of the flood is followed immediately by the saga of Nimrod and his challenge to God by building the Tower of Babel. The account of this tower was probably inspired by Babylonian architecture, but Nimrod is a direct borrowing from the personality of the demi-god, Gilgamesh – and it is to Gilgamesh that Utnapishtim, the Sumerian Noah, gives his account of how God called him to build a boat to save enough seed of the living for life to recommence after the flood.

Gilgamesh experienced a great many adventures in his search for eternal life[6] – immortality having been removed from humanity after its fall from grace in the Garden of Eden, the story of which precedes that of Noah's flood by a mere two chapters in the Book of Genesis. The closeness of the Genesis story to key aspects of the Gilgamesh legend is striking. Although the epic of Gilgamesh is four thousand years old, the idea of Utnapishtim's building a great boat was not fanciful. The explorer, Wilfred Thesiger, studied and travelled in the reed boats used by the Marsh Arabs in Iraq, built from designs and techniques that were ancient.[7] And recent explorers have completed sea crossings in a reed ship built along ancient Egyptian lines.[8] But Utnapishtim's boat, while using reeds, was made also of timber. It was two hundred feet long, wide and high – so indeed an ark or a floating chest – with seven floors of nine compartments each. The biblical ark is longer but less wide and high. The Sumerian version could have held far more species of animals.

The Gilgamesh legend probably also helped inspire elements in Homer's *Odyssey*, particularly the confrontation between Odysseus and the cyclops – which echoes Gilgamesh's conflict with Humbaba, a monstrous creature who preyed on human beings; the decapitation of Humbaba is also echoed by Perseus's beheading of Medusa. All this is to say that foundation legends spread through time in different forms, and the entire region of Mesopotamia was not only cosmopolitan in terms of interactions within its component parts but in contact with the wider worlds of Europe and Asia. In all this, the Israelites were part of great discursive exchanges that finally concretised after release from Babylon.

JUDAISM

We earlier mentioned Freud's question as to whether Moses was an Egyptian. He is a key figure in all three of the great religions of the Book, all those with a central authoritative text. Abraham as a literal sire is already problematic as his two sons, born problematically late in his life, were destined to multiply into the Israelites, on the one hand, and the Arabian nations, on the other. Jews, Christians and Islamic believers all have a common origin. But it was Moses who led the salvation of the Hebrews from servitude in Egypt. He was the instrument by which God chose them, singled them out. He led them, through many ordeals and frustrations, to become a nation. But Moses, though Hebrew by birth, was raised as an Egyptian. The story of his adoption by an Egyptian princess after he was hidden in the reeds meant not only an Egyptian but also a courtly upbringing. As a young adult, he wandered into the Hebrew quarters and, upon seeing one of the Hebrews being bullied by an Egyptian, killed the Egyptian. He thought his act had been unseen, but the next day, wandering in the same quarters, he tried to break up a fight between two Hebrews. Their response was withering: 'And who are you? I suppose you think you are our prince and judge? And will you want to kill me like you killed that Egyptian yesterday?'

Many centuries later, as the Christian era was beginning, the first Christian martyr, Stephen, was being tried before his execution. He pointedly referred to this statement of non-recognition – 'Who are you?' – referencing it to the non-recognition he himself was now receiving as a preacher. But back to the incident in Egypt, knowing that his crime had been observed, Moses fled to the land of Midian where, seemingly unable to avoid getting into fights, he rescued seven girls fetching water after they had been attacked by shepherds. Moses then helped the girls water their flocks. When the girls returned earlier than normal to their father, he asked what had happened. 'An Egyptian defended us against the shepherds'. The father, Jethro, the priest of Midian, adopted Moses into his family and he married one of the daughters.[9] But this meant that Moses looked like an Egyptian, knew nothing about Hebrew life, knew nothing about Hebrew faith and religion – although that was clearly still forming in the era before liberation, nationhood, the Ten Commandments and the religious laws of the new nation. He would have learned about the faith of the Egyptians. Indeed, Stephen in his defence described Moses as having been 'taught all the wisdom of the Egyptians, and he became a mighty prince and orator'.[10] In marriage to the daughter of the priest of Midian, he would also have learned the faith of the Midianites, and this was ironic as, many years later, one of the nations opposed to the young Hebrew state was Midian[11] – so that when God appeared to him in the burning bush to send him back to Egypt, Moses had no idea who this God was.

This is slightly to labour a point, but it is important as the exodus from Egypt, led by Moses, and the advent of the Hebrews in Canaan, their conquest of the inhabitants already there and the establishment of their own settlements and cities, signalled the creation of the precursor to today's

Israeli state. The process was also the gradual creation of a Jewish religion and ethos, not finalised until the release from Babylon many centuries later. The entire process took time, from the judges – early Israel was a confederation of tribes bound together by the interpretation of justice and righteous behaviour enunciated by judges – to the early kingdom of Saul and David, created as an organisational safeguard against rival kingdoms such as that of the Philistines, to its expansion by Solomon, not only by conquest but also by diplomatic marriages and visibly and governmentally consolidated by Solomon's construction of the first great temple, something of grandeur that finally marked a country with a metropolitan centre and a centre of learning personified in Solomon's wisdom. It was eclectic, borrowing forms of public administration from others, and was something begun by a foreigner to such identity as the captive Hebrews in Egypt had. It wasn't, at that point, a national identity.

Insofar as some, though not all, historians agree – or concede – there was or could have been an event like the 'exodus', the date attracting most concurrence is 1290 BC.[12]

Leaving Egypt in 1290 didn't mean the future Israelites reached their promised land immediately. They took forty years wandering in the wilderness, partly because they were ambivalent about leaving Egypt and given to acts of disobedience and mutiny, and partly because they had to agree or be given laws to unite them – the Ten Commandments being uppermost in the Torah and biblical accounts. This means a settlement in Canaan, gradually consolidating itself as Israel, in a period that lasted only 1,250 years until the birth of Christ. Take away seventy years in Babylonian captivity, and the rebooting of Israelite nationalism afterwards – but then add back seventy years to account for the survival of the Jewish state until its destruction in AD 70 by Roman armies, and the dispersal of the Jewish peoples throughout the known world, marking the beginning of the long era of the 'wandering Jew', and there is a total period of Israelite national organisation of only 1,250 years. It is a short time on which to hinge a claim that the land 'has always been ours'. Other majority populations lived there from AD 70 until the formation of the modern Israeli state in 1948, 1,878 years later. And before the arrival of the Hebrews in 1250 BC, earlier inhabitants had established urban settlements, including a city of two to three thousand inhabitants, the ruins of which were recently discovered by Israeli archaeologists, of nine thousand years ago.[13] That there were cities in Canaan before the invasion of the Hebrews is recounted in the Bible and Torah, as the first conquest they had to make was to capture the walled city of Jericho. But, in terms of the contest of timelines, this means that organised urban populations of non-Jewish peoples have existed in the territory, without any Jewish national presence, for some ten thousand years. The claim of a modern nationalism has therefore to have a range of foundations and rationales, not all of which can be anchored in biblical history.

It is supported, of course, by recourse to biblical prophecies, as propounded and interpreted by Christian supporters of the modern nation, but this is a recourse not always taken by Israelis themselves, even in their most orthodox guise, as will be discussed below.

Firstly, however, the era of the 'wandering Jew' became well represented in European literature – not always flatteringly. In the Elizabethan era, Shakespeare's depiction of Shylock in *The Merchant of Venice* was not atypical. Greedy, grasping for money, self-serving and unable to exhibit compassion, Shakespeare's Jew was a stereotype for whom no one felt sorry. Having rejected then-crucified Jesus, the weight of enormous sin rendered the entire race beyond the pale. In Shakespeare, a black man was depicted far more favourably and certainly nobly than a Jew. *Othello* is a proper tragic hero, married to a white woman, and the interracial nature of their relationship is not at all a subject of reproach or disapproval. Mind you, at that time, in England's Protestant quarrel with Catholic Spain, Elizabeth actively sought diplomatic allies among the North African Islamic states. A portrait of the Moroccan ambassador to her court still hangs in Tate Britain. But the image of Shylock was persistent, being essentially replicated if not further exaggerated in his 'Jewish' vices by Dickens in *Oliver Twist* as Fagin, a man of greed and miserliness but also an exploiter of children. Dickens did later apologise for his depiction and edited the second half of his book, but the damage had been well done, or well maintained, by then. Probably the most favourable depiction was by Sir Walter Scott in *Ivanhoe*, where Ivanhoe rescues the Jewish merchant, Isaac, and receives great kindness from him in return, in particular, expensive armour and a battle horse so that he might contest a great tournament, disguised but able to fight for the Saxon woman he loves. Isaac's daughter, the beauteous Rebecca, is kidnapped by the villainous knight whom Ivanhoe had defeated, and Ivanhoe, despite being wounded, risks his life to save hers. Nevertheless, Ivanhoe weds his blonde Saxon aristocrat and the raven-haired Rebecca, implicitly broken-hearted, retires – implicitly also converted – to a convent. To a huge extent, this was as good as it got.

This kind of stereotype was replicated in all the literatures of Europe. And the image of the Jew as somehow at least grubby and menial, rich by all means but certainly not at the peak of, for instance, artistic or indeed literary creation and brilliance, lasted even into the 1950s and early 1960s in the United States. Despite recognition of the terrors of the Holocaust, a residual discrimination, certainly condescension, was in place. Jews were all right, provided they also knew their place. The explosion of Jewish creative talent came only later in the 1960s. The dazzling writer Susan Sontag, herself

Jewish, broke a mould. Her biographer, Benjamin Moser, wrote that, in the early 1960s, when Sontag was teaching at Columbia, the famous New York university had only just begun admitting Jews above a previously strict and limited quota. 'Many law firms and banks, fancy clubs and elegant apartment buildings, were entirely off-limits or admitted Jews only as tokens'.

> This was true, too, at the city's most prestigious university, where even Jewish scholars of international reputation were placed in decidedly secondary positions. When Lionel Trilling became the first Jew appointed to a professorship in English, his appointment was controversial, since he could not possibly understand English literature as well as a 'rooted' Anglo-Saxon.[14]

Jews were at least not confined to US ghettos – although 'Jewish districts' still seem to exist in many well-developed cities of the West. These days, perhaps, these are no more districts of safety and isolation than Chinatowns or Little Koreas; but once, the Jewish ghetto was an enforced suburb of quarantine. Even in the work of a great European writer like Gogol, even when a Jew was treated sympathetically as a person of generosity, his dwelling in the ghetto was one of repugnance.

> (Yankel, the Jew hiding the outlaw Taras Bulba in his cart) pulled into a dark, narrow back alley, called Dirt Street or Jew Street, because Jews from all over Warsaw lived there. The alley looked like a backyard that had been turned inside out. It was as if the sun never shone there. The grimy wooden houses and the masses of clothes poles sticking out their windows made the alley even darker. Here and there the red shimmer of brick glimmered through, but most of the walls were completely covered in grime. Rarely, a plastered stretch of wall high up, seized by the sun, glared with blinding whiteness. Everything lay in a jumble: pipes, rags, rotting peels, broken tubs. All the waste and refuse was thrown into the street, assailing the senses of the passersby.[15]

Gogol was describing, perhaps with exaggeration but in keeping with stereotype about Jews and the ways in which they lived, Taras being smuggled into the Warsaw Ghetto. Many years later in World War II this would be the site, somewhat transformed and modernised, of the heroic stand of Jewish defenders against overwhelming Nazi forces. It was in many ways the birth of the new image of the 'fighting Jew', which would be rapidly transposed to the new Israel. But, before then, the ghettos and the separation of much Jewish life from the Western mainstream gave rise to impulses and thought that led to modern Judaism. It was simultaneously a renaissance and a new orthodoxy.

Gogol paints a one-dimensional picture, of course – even though Yankel helps Taras, who eventually regroups his forces to conquer Warsaw. Gogol's novel does not indicate any of the policies Taras envisaged or implemented in Poland, but the Pale of Settlement, 1791 to 1917, was a very large area that straddled the Baltic states, part of Poland and stretched south to Moldova, where Jews could freely settle. They were largely not allowed permanent abode elsewhere, certainly in its early days, except in designated ghettos. But the Pale of Settlement meant a concentration of Jewish life and culture, still beset by European influences and biases, that was expansive enough to allow some ease of cultural development and cross-fertilisation of ideas and practices, even if only from one Jewish community to another. But there were Christian orthodox influences as well and broader European cultural influences. *Tevye and His Daughters* or *Tevye the Dairyman* written by Sholem Aleichem in 1894 – later adapted for the 1964 hit Broadway musical and 1971 film, *Fiddler on the Roof*, depicted a rich and complex cultural environment in which all the same Tevye's daughters have rebellious ideas drawn from wider Europe. Aleichem wrote in Yiddish, and it is in this vernacular language of the European Jews that new thought began to be expressed and debated at community level.

Yiddish probably began being used from the ninth century, but it was, for many years, a language in development and refinement. It allowed, simultaneously, a sense of Europeanness and uniqueness. It was essentially a Germanic language with borrowings and inflections from Hebrew, Aramaic (Syriac) and some Slavic sources. However, it was written with the Hebrew alphabet. It became the dominant language of European Jews so that, before the Holocaust, it had eleven to thirteen million speakers. Of those who died in the Holocaust, 85 per cent spoke the language. Despite the decimation of the Yiddish-speaking population during World War II, the language is still spoken in Jewish orthodox and ultra-orthodox communities where, with the religious beliefs and customs of these groups, it is the language of faith. The Haredi orthodoxy, and its subgroup of the Hasidic Jews, were movements that gained ground and influence especially in the eighteenth century – and the formal dress still closely associated with them, the black coats and hats for the men, the covered hair (often covered by a wig) of the women, derives from this time. The dress of the men was, in fact, a deliberate styling, both of uniqueness and independence, but also modelled on the dress of Polish nobility. The long sideburns were a derivative of instruction from the Talmud, a body of writings discussed below, to leave the corners of the head unshaven. The complete look was therefore both an expression of pride in being a particular form of European and pride in being Jewish. The European side of things is now dated, but the Jewish nature of the identity thus depicted has strengthened. That Jewish nature, insofar as orthodoxy becomes synonymous with a form of Jewishness, is strengthened by consolidating rituals and texts.

THE ORTHODOX TEXTS

The Talmud is basically a body of laws and theological precepts that, after the destruction of the temple by the Romans in AD 70, and the dispersal of the Jews from any central state authority of their own, functioned as a unifying device. Usually divided into two epochs of compilation, the Jerusalem Talmud, dating from about AD 200, and the Babylon Talmud, from about AD 400 to 500, it is together a lengthy document with some cross-referencing of one to the other – with the Jerusalem edition having more to do with land use, looking back to a geographical state that no longer existed – and the Babylon edition almost not at all. Together, however, the unifying methodology is not only the propounding of laws and regulatory lifestyle but also the use of the opinions of learned rabbis – there obviously being more of such opinions in the later Babylonian edition. This is a direct fidelity to earlier temple methodology, where the oral teaching and preaching of the rabbi was the means of transmission of godly learning. Having said that, because literacy remained very far from universal, or even common, it meant that rabbis eventually read from and propounded legal and behavioural doctrine from the Talmud. In a way it meant the end of originality and the commencement of almost two millennia of recitative fidelity to, certainly by the twentieth century, antique codes. In a clear way, there is an analogy to be made to Islamic sharia which, nevertheless, continued to evolve until the end of the Ottoman Empire; together with Islamic hadith, laws of which the Prophet would have approved, based on observations of his teaching; and the sayings of the Islamic ulama, wise men who interpreted law and doctrine. In the days of the ghettos and the Pale of Settlement, the Talmud was a body of writings that ensured not so much fidelity as solidarity and unity of a dispersed and marginalised people. More than anything, it bound together a Jewish identity that, throughout the centuries of dispersals into many lands and miscegenation with many peoples, was able to maintain itself as an identifiable whole. Thus, a white American Jew, a more fully Semitic-appearing Middle Eastern Jew and an Ethiopian Falasha Jew will be able to establish at least something of a recognisable commonality and, within a modern Israeli state – albeit with sometimes huge tensions, for example, racism against Falashas – appear at least to be a common citizenry beyond the mere fact of living in the same space. Israel may have certain origins as a state in secular drives, but the origins of those drives were doctrinal.

The Torah is what Christians recognise as the Pentateuch, the first five books of the Old Testament, or what is referred to as the 'written' Torah, there being an extended oral series of appendices. In short, it refers to the origins of Israel until just before the Hebrew entry into Canaan and the conquest of Jericho, tracing the line of descent to Noah and backwards from there to

Adam. But the laws of the nation freed from Egypt, in the three final books, are what were probably written back by Ezra's nationalist project, depicting them as the original laws of a freed but regulatory state. The Torah is normally read with doctrinal interpretation, hence the importance of the Talmud.

There are two more texts that should be briefly mentioned. The first is the Kabbalah, a mystical set of documents of some luminosity, dating in written form from the twelfth to thirteenth centuries in Spain and the south of France – although its proponents claim an antediluvian origin. It deals with the relationship between humanity and God, something that has bewildered and fascinated people since the legends of Azael and Shemhazai's descent from heaven to woo and wed the daughters of men. Lawrence Durrell, in his *Alexandria Quartet*, featured a Kabbalist who lived in a world of ritual and mathematical mysticism.[16] This mysticism forms an esoteric undercurrent to modern Judaism but reinforces the sense of a special relationship with God.

The Haggadah, written anytime between 200 BC and AD 200 – there is dispute about the dating – is a text read primarily at Passover, giving an account of the liberation from Egypt, and is studded with blessings, prayers, moral stories and histories drawn from the Torah. Its importance is largely ceremonial and has, perhaps, a real purpose in spacing out the drinking of the cups of wine during the Passover meal but, again, reinforces the sense of a chosen deliverance by God of a special people. It follows the form of an ancient Greek symposium and is meant to be the instruction of an older generation to the young – an instruction to do with origin and being blessed at the time of origin.

But, despite these orthodox and ceremonial teachings becoming part of European Jewry, complete with a unique language of Yiddish, as time passed, a secular vision of reestablishing a nation for the Jews began to develop. This built on the religiously founded senses of identity to be sure, but it reflected the growth of modern statehood after the Treaty of Westphalia in 1648, the idea of a modern state with liberties that was a feature of the English Revolution in the seventeenth century – complete with Milton's account of rebellion against the established order and the refusal of subjugation – and the sweeping accomplishments of Napoleon's military and constitutional march across Europe from the end of the eighteenth century into the nineteenth. Theodor Herzl born was 1860, when the beginning of his modern world was within living memory.

ZIONISM

Herzl was, in many respects, a product of his times. In recounting the following synopsis of his life, I have been guided by the discriminating and perceptive comments of the former Oxford professor of Israel studies, Derek Penslar.[17] Professor Penslar begins:

> The most obvious context was the anti-Semitism that flourished in *fin de siècle* Europe. There is a famous legend that Herzl was transformed into a Zionist by the trial of Alfred Dreyfus in 1894. It is true that Herzl covered the trial as the Paris correspondent of the most influential newspaper in central Europe, *Die Neue Freie Presse*, but the trial in and of itself did not make him a Zionist. Rather, Herzl was deeply perturbed by European anti-Semitism in the early 1890s.

I do think, however, that notwithstanding the backdrop of anti-Semitism, the Dreyfus case, involving a false charge of treason, was an outstanding example of it. It was a *cause celebre* throughout Europe. Zola published his famous article, 'J'accuse', because of it, lamenting the miscarriage of justice that clearly hinged on Dreyfus being a Jew. The case may not have caused Herzl to become a Zionist but could only have been a catalysing factor amidst a general background of discrimination. As a student at the University of Vienna, suffering taunts there, Herzl flirted with the idea of revolution. This is a common enough recourse of idealistic or outraged students, but Herzl soon deduced that there would be no support among the left for Jewish emancipation – the left, despite fine words of an equal and classless society, being as immersed in discrimination as any other section of society.

He then flirted with the idea of mass conversion. If all Jews became Christians, there would be no more discrimination. But this was clearly impractical and also a removal of one of the key markers of identity and community among the Jews. As Penslar writes:

> He then fell into a kind of ecstatic state in the spring of 1895 while in Paris and he began to write constantly. Out of the mess of stuff he wrote, some of it mad, much of it quite lucid, came the material for a pamphlet which was published in 1896 and titled *The Jewish State*.

It was this piece of writing, born at the end of a period of reverie, that established the goal of Zionism – and that was the fixing of identity to a geographical homeland. Herzl didn't invent Zionism; there had been groups using the name 'Zion' since 1884, and 'Zionist' since the early 1890s; but Zion as a location was what Herzl brought to the mix. He used the term 'state', but this was not well defined – it could have been an autonomous province in either Europe or within the Ottoman Empire; it could have been a protectorate – that is, someone else's colony – but with the proviso of self-government; it could have been in Argentina, where there were Jewish agricultural settlements. But the essential obfuscation of the meaning of the word 'state' would long linger as a political device, and the terminology of a 'Jewish homeland' reflected as much a goal as a disguise to prevent panic on the part of existing states or territories. The First Zionist Congress of 1897 called for a 'national home' secured and recognised under international law. The identification of its location as Palestine came later, and the deliberate usage of the word 'state' began to be used in World War II as the depredations of the Holocaust were becoming known. Then, the idea of homeland and state were fused with the idea of refuge, and the location of Palestine gave a sense of history, antiquity and ancestry. It was the land of the forefathers from which the Jews had been evicted. All religious thought had fixated on the Jewish history in this land, including its sense of glorious history. Its regulatory frameworks, as enunciated and officialised from the time of Ezra, were still observed to one degree or another in European Jewish society. A state with a metropolitan centre, where Solomon built the first metropolitan centrepiece, the first temple, seemed a poetic justice and recompense for suffering never previously experienced in any recorded history. And it was certainly recorded, as subsequent trials for war crimes testified. Hannah Arendt's famous 'banality of evil' description of Eichmann's minute recordings of executions and terrors further unveiled what had been known since at least the earlier Nuremberg trials: good bureaucrats industriously recorded an industrial process of mass execution extending into the millions.[18]

There were only two problems with the idea of homeland and refuge and history: the first was that someone else lived in Palestine; There were roughly seven hundred thousand Arab inhabitants and a minority population of fifty-eight thousand Jews – some part descended from the tiny residue the Romans left behind and some who settled during the time of the Ottomans; the second was that the British had mandate rights over it. But those rights were acquired as a result of World War I in the war against the Ottoman Empire – where the legendary 'Lawrence of Arabia' championed the cause of the Arabs and led them to support the British. Promises, far from fully fulfilled, were made to the Arabs, but the British – now cognisant of a growing Zionist movement - did contemplate what to do for the Jews. In 1917, a year before the end of World War I, Lord Balfour, the British foreign secretary, sent a letter to Lord Rothschild, a prominent member of the Jewish community in London and well connected to Zionist groups. It was a typical gentlemanly letter – some legends suggest it was delivered in person in the Reform Club in Pall Mall, the quintessential stuffy gentlemen's club – and it was, in the light of its consequences, amazingly brief. It used the term, 'national home', not 'state', and made a caveat – never honoured, at least never rigorously attempted to be honoured – about protection of the rights of the Arab population. And, notwithstanding the recognition of a growing Zionist movement, it was also to secure Jewish community support for the remaining British war effort and, probably above all, pave the way for help from the Jewish community and

Jewish bankers like Rothschild to finance the huge economic cost of having waged four years of international war.

November 2nd, 1917

Dear Lord Rothschild,

I have much pleasure in conveying to you, on behalf of His Majesty's Government, the following declaration of sympathy with Jewish Zionist aspirations which has been submitted to, and approved by, the Cabinet. 'His Majesty's Government view with favour the establishment in Palestine of a national home for the Jewish people, and will use their best endeavours to facilitate the achievement of this object, it being clearly understood that nothing shall be done which may prejudice the civil and religious rights of existing non-Jewish communities in Palestine, or the rights and political status enjoyed by Jews in any other country'. I should be grateful if you would bring this declaration to the knowledge of the Zionist Federation.

Yours sincerely,

Arthur James Balfour[19]

With such a brief letter, historical change (some would say historical infamy) began. Even so, it took another world war to act as the final push to the creation of today's Jewish state. This is not to say that the Zionist movement abated – it increased – and there was anticipatory Jewish migration to Palestine, but the terrible events of war propelled events forwards, both in movements towards a homeland in Palestine and then Jewish seizure of the moment to force the issue after the war's end. Before then, however, history saw the height of anti-Semitism in Germany and many other parts of Europe. This started several years before the war, as recounted in Fred Uhlman's brief but elegantly tragic only semi-fictionalised memoir of a Jewish schoolboy in Stuttgart.[20] It extended, during the war, well beyond the borders of Germany, as related by the Croatian historian, Slavko Goldstein[21] – who, as a teenage Jewish schoolboy went into the mountains to fight with Tito's partisans. And, of course, the concentration camps themselves evoked heroically plangent memories, notably those by Primo Levi.[22] Levi was at pains to write also about Jewish resistance. Small groups of guerrilla fighters assembled and resisted as best they could in the forests.[23] Levi himself fought in one such group before being captured and sent to Auschwitz. Daniel Craig's 2008 film, *Defiance*, is about such a guerrilla band fighting in occupied Belarus. But the idea, the image, of the 'fighting Jew' was most stood large in the heroic stand of the Warsaw Ghetto, some of whose few survivors escaped to join the guerrilla bands.

The uprising in the Warsaw Ghetto occurred in 1943, after a quarter of a million Jews had already been seized from the area and sent to the camps.

But the uprising was doomed from the start. Despite smuggling in arms and deploying themselves as best they could against overwhelming German forces, the aim was not to defeat the Germans or even greatly delay an inevitable fate – rather to welcome that fate. As Marek Edelman, the only surviving commander, said, it was "to pick the time and place of our deaths". Thirteen thousand Jews died, against less than twenty German deaths. However, the photographs that emerged from the conflict, with men and women fighting ferociously side by side, created a legend.[24] Coming relatively late in the war, it created a template for Jewish military resolve after the war.

But the impact of what greeted the eyes of allied soldiers liberating the camps meant that their political leaders, particularly British leaders who had subscribed to the Balfour Declaration, could not any longer delay the project of a homeland. It was to be a creation of homeland that was handled both badly and violently, encountering great resistance from the Palestinian population, and massive conflict with the surrounding Arab states.

ENDLESS WARS: THE MILITARISED STATE

The biblical accounts in Judges, Kings and Chronicles of constant war between Israel and surrounding states echo in these modern times. The relative stability of Solomon's great kingdom was also when Israel briefly reached its greatest geographical extent – this extent lasting probably less than thirty years – but the then unmeasured and inexact borders of his country form the circumference for the *eretz* Israel, the ancient biblical Israel, that are used as justification for today's expansionist state with its far more precise territorial goals. Solomon of course did not rely on war, but more on diplomacy. His many marriages were to cement diplomatic alliances. King Hiram of Tyre, a city that still exists in Lebanon, sent cedars from Lebanon to help build David's palace, and then to help his son, Solomon, build the temple. It seems from non-biblical sources that Hiram and Solomon collaborated to build a merchant shipping route through the Red Sea which allowed trade with countries as far away as the Philippines. But diplomacy, political or economic, was in short supply at the birth of today's Israel. This was certainly not all the fault of new migrant Jewish communities, anxious to kick-start the process of statehood, but was also down to British and then United Nations (UN) mismanagement, or inability to manage, the rapidly increasing pace of events. The Palestinians put up their own ferocious resistance both to the British and to the incursion of Jewish communities.

From 1922, Britain had held the League of Nations mandate for Palestine. In 1947, Britain announced it would return the mandate to the League's successor organisation, the United Nations. In November of that year, the UN agreed the partition of Palestine, and the British expressed their intention of ending their mandate by May 1948, and to withdraw their military forces as soon as possible thereafter. The figures used at that time are very interesting. The Jewish 'state' or homeland would occupy 56 per cent of the area of Palestine, and have a population of 499,000 Jews, but also 510,000 Arabs. The Palestinian state, 43 per cent of the territory, would have a population of 747,000 Arabs, and 10,000 Jews. Jerusalem and Bethlehem would be UN-administered territories, totalling only sixty-eight square miles, with about 100,000 Jews and 100,000 Arabs. The numbers, in terms of most nations, never mind two, were tiny, and the size of the territories themselves was also tiny. People who have never been to Israel and Palestine, notwithstanding the changing borders as a result of wars and annexations, have no idea about the miniscule scale for which war has been waged. This in itself makes conflict 'understandable' – never mind scriptural promises of entitlement. Land is a scarce commodity. There is very little to go around. But the Arab population figures were based on actual population at the time, and with 13 per cent less accorded land, the number of Arabs was greater than the number of Israelis by 60 per cent. Just in numerical terms, the partition seemed a great injustice to the Arab population. At the same time, given that the territory accorded to the Jews under the partition was meant to solve the 'Jewish question' in Europe, the amount of territory in its then undeveloped state could scarcely have accommodated a fraction of surviving European Jewry, numbering about 3.5 million. Even so, even the prospect of more than half a million Jews permanently settled in the region – a huge rise from the 58,000 at the beginning of the century – seemed to the surrounding Arab states a fundamental reshaping of the demographics and culture of the Middle East with its hitherto (difficult) homogeneity and, regional pronunciations notwithstanding, common language and, above all, religious customs.

Militarised resistance to the Jews began, with Palestinian militias augmented by other Arab volunteers. Jewish convoys and isolated villages were key targets. Ben Gurion, who had emerged as the leader of the Jewish communities in Palestine, issued a stand-fast order – no village was to evacuate, and none did. But the violence greatly unsettled the British who became simultaneously anxious to leave but reluctant to extend a full handover to the UN. This was partly because the UN itself was embroiled in fierce debate occasioned by its Arab members but, as arguments raged in New York, things got worse on the ground as Jewish forces began pre-emptive attacks – often against innocent targets. The Palestinian and Arab forces intensified their own responses and things began slipping out of everyone's control with the appearance of Jewish terrorist gangs, determined to take the law – such as it was – into their own hands. The advent of the Stern Gang and the Irgun (led by future Israeli Prime Minister Menachim Begin) was an ominous development. Together, in one attack, they wiped out some 254 Arabs, including women and children at prayer, and exhibited the 150 survivors as trophies. Gradually the Jewish forces – not without further atrocities and terror attacks, notably the Irgun's 1946 blowing up of the King David Hotel, site of the British administration in Jerusalem, with ninety-one dead – turned the tide and the UN, its administration finally in place, was witness to the mass exodus of tens of thousands of Palestinians whose towns and villages had been conquered by the Jewish forces.

On 14 May 1948, Ben Gurion, flush with military triumphs, declared the independence of Israel as a state. President Truman of the United States immediately recognised Israel, throwing his own negotiators at the UN into surprise and fury that such a unilateral action had occurred and been sanctioned. The Arab response was trenchant, and the new state of Israel entered its existence confronted by foreign armies ready to move against it from all sides.[25]

This is not the place to recount each of the great Arab–Israeli wars that took place – the war following independence in 1948, the incursion into Suez in 1956, the stunning and overwhelming Israeli victory in the June war of 1967, the reversal of some Israeli gains by the Egyptians in Sinai in 1973 – plus all the subsequent incursions into Lebanon and Gaza. These have been minutely described, dissected and analysed by many others and from many points of view.[26] What I want to analyse at this juncture is the thought processes that developed in the war for independence and the wars that followed, notwithstanding various peace talks and the radical diplomatic initiative of Egyptian President Sadat, visiting Israel in 1977, followed by the Camp David accords between Sadat and Begin in 1978, and which finally resulted in a peace treaty in 1979 and diplomatic relations between Egypt and Israel at the beginning of 1980. This effort at *rapprochement* did not, however, change the intellectual and ideological direction of Israeli thought – to which, over the forty years since 1980, should be added greater religious influence, the move towards annexation of further Palestinian territory, and the development of an existential unease over a homeland for the Jews, where the Jews might eventually be outnumbered by Palestinians without rights – a homeland with its own built-in structure for undermining itself.

THE DEVELOPMENT OF THOUGHT

The ruthlessness of terrorist gangs in the independence struggle revealed the existence of a range of thought in the nascent Israeli body politic. A left wing idealism, seeking a modern state with modern citizenship rights and benefits, was contrasted with a sense of brutal superiority, considering the Palestinians as second-class beings, as disposable – a form of proto-fascism which, at the very least, was tragically ironic, given what fascism had done to the Jews, treating them precisely as disposable and, with an industrial machine, setting about to make them so. The ingredients of the future Israeli state did not have a German industrial capacity, but the new state soon achieved rapid militarisation and an advanced sense of military strategy – again, ironically, borrowed from German strategists like Guderian and the application of Clausewitz's dictum to his Panzer forces, ascertaining the enemy's weakest point, mobilising at greater speed than the enemy can match, and smashing your way in great force at that weakest point; this was used with devastating effect particularly in the 1967 war, where Israeli tanks simply sliced apart Egyptian formations at every single weak point.[27] But, with a constantly alert military machine, and in a young society with senior commanders achieving elite status in society when no longer in uniform, but where with constant call-up and reserve status blurring the line between military and civilian life in any case, the virtues of military doctrine permeated civilian policy formation. Former terrorist leaders, generals and officers, took their turns as prime minister of Israel. Some were decidedly liberal – if not obviously so to the subjugated Palestinian population – but others were hawkish in or out of uniform. Colin Shindler has written about how Zionism achieved an operational military dimension, and how the militarisation of Zionism became part of the doctrine of post-independence Israel.[28] Shindler associates much of this with political parties like the Likud and its long-time leader, Prime Minister Netanyahu.[29]

This view is also expressed eloquently by Avi Shlaim.[30] Rafael Behr's review of his book is more abrupt in its rendition of Likud than even Shlaim's writing:

He means a configuration of history that casts one side of a dispute as victim and the other as aggressor in the eyes of the world.

In Zionism's case, the story told is of Israel restored to the Jews from antiquity, carved from empty desert, 'a land without a people for a people without a land'. By extension, Arab hostility to Israel's creation was irrational cruelty directed against an infant state.

It is a romantic myth requiring a big lie about the indigenous Palestinian population. Their expropriation was, in Shlaim's analysis, the 'original sin' that made conflict inevitable. He also sees the unwillingness of Israeli leaders to recognise the legitimacy of Palestinian grievance as the reason why most peace initiatives have failed.

There was a time of greater pragmatism, when ordinary Israelis at least were ready to swap land for peace. But that trend was crushed by a generation of turbo-Zionists from the Likud party. Instead of trading occupied territory for normal diplomatic relations with the Arab world, they aggressively colonised it, waging demographic war to shrink the borders and diminish the viability of any future Palestinian state.[31]

The views of these three Jewish writers, Shindler, Shlaim and Behr, themselves reflect one end of a spectrum of thought and judgement that stretches from a proto-fascism – it's ours, the others can go rot – to a trenchant condemnation of continued expansionism and annexation. All, however, defend the existence of an Israeli state, a Jewish homeland. That state once attracted immense international leftwing support through its developmental programmes based on the communal and cooperative, egalitarian and agri-technologically savvy *kibbutz* movement[32] – above all seen as a secular and socialist model.

But, insofar as left support, even endorsement of the Israeli project could be sustained, its foundations were eroded with continuing depredations of the Palestinians.[33] But what probably completed the deligitimisation of the project occurred with the first *intifada*, then the steady betrayal of the Oslo Accords, the second *intifada* that accompanied aspects of Israeli non-compliance, and the clear policy of reducing Palestinian lands to a mere emirate, leading to the border wall, with a border set within what had been Palestinian territory, and continuing settlements on what, under Oslo, was meant to be, or one day meant to be Palestinian land.

The Oslo Accords, initiated by Track II or unofficial diplomacy in Oslo, but rapidly formalised, led to agreements in 1993 and 1995. The Israelis negotiated from a position of great military strength, having expelled the Palestinian Liberation Organisation (PLO) from its headquarters in Beirut in 1982, after a highly controversial assault. There was a great anxiety within the PLO seeking to reestablish some visible and tangible presence in the region, and the Israelis saw a benefit in this as the first *intifada*, an uprising by, particularly, the young Palestinians against continued Israeli occupation of territories in the West Bank and Gaza, 1987 to 1993, resulted in repeated images of youths throwing stones and using slingshots against Israeli armoured vehicles. These echoed those of the citizens of Budapest resisting Warsaw Pact tanks with stones in 1956 and, more significantly and ironically, David confronting the huge, armoured Goliath with a slingshot. It was, at the very least, bad public relations for Israeli policy. Some 'tamed' Palestinian leadership that could control the unrest was in the Israeli interest. As it was, the PLO, led by Yasser Arafat, negotiated badly. The PLO delegation was short on legal and English-language expertise. Arafat himself seemed not to understand very well legal niceties, and the slight differences in possible interpretation between the Arab and English versions of the final Accords.[34]

What it accomplished for the PLO was the establishment of a Palestinian Authority, stationed in Ramallah on the West Bank. What this accomplished for the Israelis was to an appreciable extent a quasi 'captive' Palestinian leadership, dependent on Israeli cooperation for an entire range of economic provisions, even for water rights, but particularly for the stage-by-stage implementation of the Accords when it came to ownership and government of the land. For the Israelis, if worse came to worst, Arafat and the PLO were 'within range'. I mentioned earlier how small all of Israel and Palestine, no matter how configured, actually are. Ramallah is only half an hour's drive from Jerusalem. Arafat could both posture as a president and also be a target.

The land question was, to an extent, fudged. A small amount of Category A land would come under immediate Palestinian control. This included Ramallah – in effect a small city-state. Much other land was Category B, under joint Palestinian/Israeli control; in practice, this was much more Israeli than Palestinian control and, at the very least, gave an effective veto by the Israelis over control in this category. In due course, this category was to migrate to Category A status. It never has, and the slowness of even Israeli posturing that it might have led to a second *intifada* from 2000 to 2005. Unlike the first *intifada*, this was incited by the PLO as one of the only weapons at its disposal. Category C land, 63 per cent of the West Bank, remained under Israeli control. It too was meant to migrate to Category B status, but never did, and it was on this land that, at first, Israeli settlements multiplied – before also springing up in Category B. Most Palestinian population is in A and B, but in Category C, Jewish settlers now outnumber Palestinians. In this sense, the slow timeline proposed by Oslo gave a cloak for a creeping colonisation of Palestine, effectively rendering any final settlement – if ever there is one, but this was the substance of the proposals by President Trump in January 2020 – as the unveiling of a Palestine as a series of 'free' city-states with their hinterlands and linking roads in a non-contiguous 'state' of reduced size to that envisaged by Oslo and an entire series of negotiations over many years. Even with such reduction, if Israeli control over water rights remained, and if the Palestinians are not permitted (as now they are not permitted) an airport, Israel would control the substance of life and most of the transport links with the outer world. Palestine would be a vassal state. There is only one problem for the Israelis with this vision of control and overlordism: this geographically reduced Palestine cannot contain all the Palestinian population in the region. Many remain on Israeli territory, including any annexed territories, without Israeli citizenship rights and with nowhere else to go.

The growing numbers of such Palestinians poses a quandary for a Jewish homeland which could eventually become a homeland in which Jews are the minority population. If the Palestinians are not given full political rights, the comparison with apartheid gathers force. If given them political rights, there could be (but this would take generations of competition by birth rate), by electoral means, majority Palestinian rule over the Jewish homeland. Even if generations off, the clear and visible presence of Palestinians in Israel is a constant reminder of a rival people. This is what the Israeli scholar, Uriel Abulof, calls the great 'existential threat' faced (and feared) by Israeli Jews.

It becomes a deep securitisation drama from which there is no easy release.[35] If no easy release, and if no viable Palestinian state with full national and international rights – that is, able to refuse settlements by 'foreigners' – is subjugation to time immemorial the only path forwards? In all this quandary of superiority, what is the role of tradition and religion?

The main Haredi orthodoxy in the European Jewish population was opposed to Zionism right up to the creation of the State of Israel – and many continued their scepticism of the *bona fides* of the state because of its secularism, fearing that secular state nationalism would become a stronger unifying force for the Jewish people than religious faith. This was a fundamental point. Was what played a major role in sustaining a scattered population for more than almost two thousand years, giving all its parts a common identity, lost in less than one century? However, since about 80 per cent of the European Orthodox Jews were eliminated in the Holocaust, it took their numbers – and influence – a long time to recover, and, by then, the state of Israel was a reality. Even then, some parts of orthodoxy thought the state premature and, to an extent, presumptuous – their reading of scripture suggesting that Israel could not be restored until the appearance of the messiah. In more ways than one, Israel was taking God's matters into its own hands. The increase in orthodox migration from Europe and the United States to Israel is a relatively recent phenomenon, but the orthodox population of Israel is now about 8 per cent. Many claim (and are accorded) major exemptions from social responsibilities, such as for the defence of the state, which meant exemption from conscription and military service. This aloofness has created a clear division in Israel, with a perceived unpopularity of the Haredi in many majority streams of society.[36] All the same, rigorous observance of practices such as the Sabbath – and the cessation of economic activity on that day – means that the presence of religion and its traditions are never far away. The importance of Jerusalem – a complete city as an emblem – harks back to the importance of Solomon's Temple as the concrete unifying achievement of the biblical State of Israel. The annual celebration of Passover – the ceremony and remembrance of deliverance, of being chosen for salvation, means that even an atheist cannot escape recognition that, in recent times, the creation of the state was the creation of a land of salvation, which, all the same, still seems insecure. The very animosity of Arab populations and the Palestinians, in particular, whether provoked or not, reinforces the sense of having been saved, chosen, and of the need to defend salvation. There is even the similarity of enemies, ancient and modern, with the Palestinians cast almost into the role of the Philistines. Everywhere, the secular state relies on a backdrop of faith and history steeped in faith. And the presence in the Likud, in parliament, and fielding ministers, of minor but often decisively influential religious parties – in a state of constant coalition governments – means that all political thought must recognise the existence of religious thought, the politicisation of religion and, indeed, an inescapable religiosity within politics.

THREE CONCLUDING (BUT LARGE) FACTORS

The first is that we have spoken about the West Bank and the conditional governing of it by the Palestinian authority under the PLO; but the Israelis greatly prefer the PLO over Hamas – the rival Palestinian political party with its stronghold in Gaza, Hamas having been driven into this enclave in 2006 after Palestinian parliamentary elections, which it won, but which the PLO sought to circumvent and, with Western (and Israeli) support, did. Hamas began as a community movement, providing support on a local basis. It was, at first, inchoate in terms of an overarching programme. Even Edward Said, in Hamas's early days, thought it could not pose any serious challenge to the PLO.[37] However, its unifying force was its early Islamic foundations, and its use of religion as a fulcrum upon which to lever its opposition not only to Israeli occupation but to Israel itself. Here, the Israelis, in blockading Gaza (inadvertently demonstrating exactly how it could blockade any eventual Palestinian state) were aided and abetted by the Egyptians, seeing in Hamas allies to the Muslim Brotherhood, long an oppositional force to the hybrid military/civilian and secular regimes of Egypt. Hamas is somewhat more complex than just its Islamic points of ideological orientation[38] – its support base relies, in part, on Palestinian dissatisfaction with the PLO – but insofar as it remains within a realm of Islam that touches upon jihadism, the questions are stark and simple: What if, in the constant refusal to accord the PLO government in the West Bank, some success stories about, in particular, rights over more land, Israel stirs support for Hamas born out of frustration with the PLO? What if groups like al-Qaeda, ISIS (Islamic State of Iraq and Syria) or descendant groups finally take Palestine seriously rather than fighting against other Muslims? With ISIS-level organisation, equipment and an international fighting force, what would the consequences of a rampaging Hamas in Israel be? Would the military incursions of Israel into Gaza to punish Hamas for its homemade rocket attacks, born out of a refusal to negotiate with Hamas that echo early refusals to negotiate with the PLO, finally reap its whirlwind?[39]

The second is that Israel and Palestine are simply part of great superpower projects in the Middle East. What happens in Israel's surrounding territories will impact Israel. The US quarrel with Iran may determine the level of support it is possible for Iran to give to Lebanon's Hezbollah – a group with both genuine Lebanese political presence and parliamentary participation, and with serious military strength – which it has used against Israeli incursions with success. But the superpower interventions throughout the post–World War II period have rendered the Middle East a cauldron of sensitivities and conflicts.[40] These will not necessarily end soon, and the spectre of nuclear-armed states like Iran and Israel facing off against each other is the spectre of nuclear holocaust. The stakes in the region rise rather than fall.

The third is the realm of Israeli politics, its divisions and its saturation with the question of land. It saturates Palestinian politics too. I conclude this chapter, therefore, with a personal recollection. In 2009, I was part of a small delegation in Jerusalem received by then-Israeli deputy prime minister Dan Meridor, part of the coalition under Likud and widely regarded as a 'dove' by comparison to Prime Minister Netanyahu. The delegation comprised military generals from three countries, as well as former ambassadors, with some scholars who had backgrounds of international engagement. Altogether we were able to fit around a small conference table. Meridor had offered us a briefing on the history of the land-for-peace negotiations and, knowing that with an audience of this sort he could not talk in platitudes, went into a very straight-forward description, with maps for each stage, of the negotiations over the years. This lasted an hour and, afterwards, he assigned a colonel to show us what these maps and their lines meant in real terms. We were on a hilltop and suddenly the US general gripped me by the arm: 'Stephen! That disagreement over this area in negotiation x – the disagreement was over an area no larger than a football pitch! It's right below us! And they still couldn't agree!' Finally, how much land either side gets may pale into insignificance in the light of existential anxiety on both sides. Identity and recognisable location in the region, and only then measurable location in the region, mock mere formulae. In the case of the Jews and Judaism, and all its strands of thought and emphases from different epochs of history, we have an amazing non-formulaic story – in fact, three stories.

The nation of Israel was thrice founded: firstly in its post-Exodus settlement in Canaan, but taking time to establish full governance structures and, by implication, legal codes; secondly in its post-Babylon return to Israel, with laws, codes and their historical authentication being propounded by Ezra and the priestly legalists; thirdly in 1948, with the foundation of the current state, but with significant expansions of territory as a result of wars and regional hegemony – and with intense coalition bargaining still in place in the regular formation of hybrid governments, all concerned with the future shape and content of the country, that content being, in part, to do with the continuation and extension of historical and mythological provenance.

This means that the religious laws of the nation of Israel have been in flux, with Ezra writing forwards by abstracting from what went before, and with current debates as to who and what is a Jew. Some orthodox believers deny that migrants from Russia could be true Jews; there is racism against the Ethiopian Falashas. There is a black American group in Israel that denies that anyone else is a true Jew. Essentially, although seeming now to be in fixed abode, it is a nation still in creation.

Nevertheless, what is amazing is that after dispersal by the Romans in AD 70, and after Constantine's declaration of Christianity as the official religion of the Roman Empire in AD 325, and the persecution of the Jews as the assassins of Jesus gathered force, and Jewish communities were increasingly confined to isolated areas and separate suburbs or ghettos of cities, that culture and tradition in fact seemed to intensify over the centuries. Did the ghettos curate culture, or did culture of this sort seek and perhaps need a separated site in which to thrive and bind, solidifying a dispersed community that might otherwise have integrated with host societies much more than they did? The coherence of Jewish culture, notwithstanding arguments between the orthodox and secular, was an impressive feat.

However, the era of states, of how states should be constitutionalised, the advent of international modernity, all led to a desire to participate in the new history. The sense of discrimination never went away, even if you became a wealthy banker and ennobled as was Lord Rothschild – so that Lord Balfour, at least in courtesy terms, addressed him as an equal – and the intensity of discrimination reached its apotheosis in the Holocaust. After that, there was no turning back from the idea of a separate state, a homeland for the Jews, ringed with steel that projected outwards.

That steel is pointed inwards as well, as Palestinians would testify – so that the Israeli–Palestinian relationship poses a great contradiction in that a nation that survived ruthlessness at the hands of the Nazis is prepared to be ruthless to others.

The foundational ceremony of Israel, Passover, speaks tellingly of an angel, from a heavenly realm not far removed from human nature, who descends on God's instructions to kill children to secure the release from Egypt. God speaks and guides Moses personally. Heaven is ruthless, and heaven has a personal relationship with Israel. This is – to put it with moderate poetic exaggeration, no doubt, but even with a brief essence of such self-assurance and self-justification with a sense of separateness and chosen uniqueness – what chance is there for Israel to intersect with Others? Or will the accomplished state, perhaps with magnified borders, be a powerful ghetto among the nations of the Middle East? And ironies play out through history: it was Persia that released Israel from Babylon; today, Israel sees Iran as the foe behind all others, at least greater than all others, so that even the Palestinians are seen as cyphers in a very great game, in which a very small country must posture powerfully, court greater powers and fend off all others.

Chapter 2

The Religions of the Book
The Embodied Christ

In a curious way, Christianity is the most pervasively difficult religion in international politics. A great deal of received history in the traditionally hegemonic nations of the world has been 'Christian'. Other histories stand in relation to it as an antecedent (Judaism) or a predestined rival or even mirror image (Islam, in interpretations of the biblical account of the sons of Abraham, being the progeny of Ishmael). Only the latter-day emergence of China has disrupted this Mediterranean and transatlantic sense of Christianity as centre or as a central rival. Since the adoption of Christianity as the official creed of the Roman Empire, Jews and Judaism have been seen both as a repudiated people responsible for the crucifixion of Christ and as a redeemed grouping entitled in the 'last days' to repossess Palestine. The history of Christianity has required twin symbioses, one with the Jews and the other with Islam. The Crusades to reclaim the Holy Land from Islam, the confrontation between Islamic and Christian kingdoms in Spain, the designation of the Holy Roman Empire, the confrontation in years afterwards with the Ottoman Empire and today's discourse of Islamic insurgency, all speak of a simultaneous Christian and binary character to the foundations of Western history. The Christian character has infused even modern governments. Bishops still sit as 'Lords Spiritual' in the British House of Lords. Every US president ends his State of the Union address with the words, 'God bless America', and President Trump's 2019 address laboured the point that Americans were born in the image of God. His support from the 'Christian right' suggests that any full secularism is far from the heart of US politics. Yet, if the United States remains at least constitutionally secular, while inescapably religious in its political rhetoric, the outreach of Christianity to the non-Mediterranean and non-Atlantic world in the former colonies of European powers is immense. Zambia is now constitutionally a Christian nation and, despite all manner of efforts to reclaim and decolonise history, the one greatest impact of colonialism, Christianity in mainstream, evangelical or miscegenated forms, seems set to stay and indeed grow stronger. But it is in Europe, now buffeted by tides of refugees that we see a turn to closures and closed borders where right-wing politics are most fervently tied to a preservation of 'Christian values' and a 'Christian way of life'. All of this is to suggest a united purpose and closure of the historical schism within Christianity between Catholic and Protestant/Orthodox, yet it is far from dead as evidenced in the inability of Northern Ireland to join Ireland, in the Orthodox and Catholic distinctions between Serbia and Croatia – where religion played a role in politics and individual nation-building in the wake of the federal union of Yugoslavia. Within the inside/outside binary, lies a binary in the inside.

It is not possible in one, even extended, chapter to do justice to all of this. What I shall try to do here is certainly to look at the binary between Catholicism and Protestantism, but particularly to look at the binary between literalness and luminosity, between human embodiment and spiritual release, between darkness and light.

PROLOGUE

If one wanders the old streets of Addis Ababa, and this had better now be done sooner rather than later as the city rapidly transforms itself into a modern metropolis, one comes across a district called Somali Town, with streets of stalls selling everything from car parts; you can get a crankshaft made to measure and heat-stressed from backyard furnaces and lathes, or you can buy naïve art, almost always depicting two key themes. The first is of the Queen of Sheba, 'Magda' in the local legends, where she is depicted as an Ethiopian, going to the Court of Solomon not to marvel at the king's wisdom but to test his wisdom against her own. A fierce equality is suggested here. The second is of the battle of Adwa, fought in 1896, where the Ethiopian army defeated the Italian army seeking to spearhead the colonisation of a country that remained stubbornly – as the rest of Africa fell to European powers – independent. Both sides are matched in armaments, rifles and cannons, but both sides also evacuate their wounded to Red Cross tents. In the heavens, however, St George and the angels fight with the Ethiopians, and they are not white. Christianity became the state religion of Ethiopia in AD 330, under the Ethiopian Coptic Christian Church. What we now know as Roman Catholicism was established by a series of councils, starting with the Council of Nicaea in 325, with its foundational doctrine refined by the

Council of Constantinople in 381, but with final agreement on liturgy only in 692. Although it is a close-run thing – a matter of five years – as to which state, Ethiopia or Rome, first adopted and officialised Christianity (and both were probably beaten by Armenia in 301) the Ethiopian liturgy in fact pre-dates officialisation and can lay claim to being the oldest liturgical tradition and, by that measure, claim also to be the closest to the apostolic liturgy and ceremonial practices developed after the death of Jesus for the early spread of the church. The key element in all this returns to the artwork, not just of naïve painters in today's streets but of the ancient church murals in Ethiopia – where Jesus and the heavenly hosts are black.

They are stubbornly white in Northern Atlantic Christianity and in all the missionary-disseminated branches of Christianity throughout the rest of Africa. Zambia made Christianity the state religion in 1996 but, in all its mainstream and most of the smaller Pentecostal and Apostolic churches, the artistic depictions, particularly of the crucified Christ, depict a white man with flowing, non-dreaded hair.

The embodiment of Christ, either as a baby freshly born in a stable or as a dead man freshly executed, bookend a life in which a full range of human attributes are conferred upon him, including despair in the Garden of Geth-semane, courage before Pilate, endurance while being tortured and agony while dying. Only of eros and sex was he denied in the Gospel accounts, but that was remedied in the host of alternative narratives of his life from the Gnostic Gospels to the mystic legends of the Holy Grail and the marriage to Mary Magdalene. It was as if he could never be made too human, and it was desirable that he be made so – a Christ able to be appropriated because he was made into enough of a non-God to absorb human empathy as a key form of worship.

Almost as an antidote, angels began acquiring wings around AD 300, pos-sibly under Persian influence – and there is a full range of possible Persian influences, chiefly from the Zoroastrian-descendant cult of Mithras to which frontline Roman soldiers were exposed, ranging from the virgin birth to the flight into Egypt, not to mention the constant struggle between light and dark – but the advent of wings helped ensure the place of angels as intermediaries between heaven and earth; they were a bit of both.[1] Their becoming either androgynous or female by Renaissance times was paralleled by their fallen counterparts having become demonic and lizard-like. But these female angels were creatures of purity, virginal, and again represented an aspirational state beyond most human capacity. Only the Christ was born, lived, suffered and died as a human being. It is this Christ – able to lead the way to elevation from direct knowledge of our own condition – who blesses soldiers about to suffer and die in battle for nations embodied in his name.

CHRISTIANITY: THE EASE OF THE LITERAL

When we speak of Judaism, we speak of peoples lately made into one nation. When we speak of Christianity, we speak in global terms of its acceptance or rejection in many nations. It has been present everywhere. Even Israel benefits from a huge Christian tourist industry where visitors flock to see Bethlehem and the Mount of Olives and create the spectacle of lugging (usually balsa wood) crosses around the streets of the Old City of Jerusalem, imagining they are trudging in the steps of Jesus. They are not, of course, as this is the Ottoman city – but anything that looks old must be ancient. And they make their pilgrimage to the Valley of Megiddo, where the Book of Revelation prophesied that history will end with the last battle between God's and Satan's armies as numberless as the sands of the seashore. They will have to fit into forty-seven acres – although, realising this, many Christian commentators have extended the area immensely to accommodate armies like grains of sand. The literalness of much Christian faith is an element that belies the metaphorical and poetic qualities of Aramaic, the language of Jesus and the Gospels.[2] The choice of interpretation, whether literal or metaphorical, lies at the heart of much Christian dispute, most apparent in the United States in English – a language famed, outside of its best literature, for its austerity when it comes to poetic suggestibility.

Two significant religions have been founded in the United States: the first is the Church of Jesus Christ of Latter-Day Saints, with emphasis on the word 'latter', and its Book of Mormon is subtitled 'Another Testament of Jesus Christ'; and the second is Scientology, begun in the 1950s by science fiction writer L. Ron Hubbard. The first fulfils two needs: (1) of a literal history without the metaphors of a biblical book like Revelation and (2) of a desire for a record of physical presence by Christ on American soil. The land is as it were blessed by physical touch. The second, Scientology, brings a curious space-age popularisation and vulgarisation of science: it imparts a rationality to the unexplained – the external forces of other religious texts, heavenly spirits, are rendered as visitors from outer space, beneficent aliens, and utilises a simplified proto-science in its 'dianetics', a belief system in which the soul was preincarnated in other parts of the universe, and in which the measurement of electrical currents through one's body can help in what is claimed to be a diagnosis of mental health.[3] So, if one religion seeks a validation by looking back, even inventing back, the other situates itself firmly within claims of scientific modernity and looking to physical worlds beyond the earth. Together they represent almost the conscious American ambition to escape religion as luminosity, as capable of spirituality, by anchoring it to literalness and 'science'.

Certainly, the epic narratives of the Book of Mormon are a direct recasting of biblical accounts of wars and struggle for land – but set in America. The sagas of the Nephites, Lamanites and Jaredites are akin to those of the tribes and people of the Old Testament seeking a land. Huge battles are fought, and huge stone cities are built and destroyed. All is resolved when Jesus comes to walk the land. The illustrations to modern editions are very, what we would now call, 'socialist realist' (the same style of art is used in the Hare Krishna editions of the Bhagavad Gita, where Krishna lives among men as a charioteer, and in North Korean books depicting the life of Kim Il Sung, a demi-god among men) – that is, depicting, without scope for misinterpretation, something almost photographically literal. My own edition of the Book of Mormon, almost as if to compensate for the lack of archaeological ruins to substantiate the sagas of great cities, has a picture of Jesus walking among Aztecs with their pyramids in the background. He is a longhaired white man, showing them his stigmata. Thankfully, all others are brownish, though with square jaws and chiselled features. Reportedly discovered on engraved plates by Joseph Smith in 1830, their location revealed by an angel to him, his publication of their contents began very quickly to amass a huge following. The prophecies in the book point to a great nation, provided it kept fidelity to God, and Smith himself pointed to his vision of a theo-democracy, an amalgam of Christian faith (it didn't have to be Mormon) and secular democracy. The combination reflected the developing vision of the United States as a whole.

What it points to is a nation-state of such greatness it is a beacon to the world – but its faith is literal rather than luminous. The sign-off line, almost the signature of every presidential State of the Union address is 'God bless America'. It brings an authority to the union and to the president himself.[4] At the same time, God is imagined with great powers but human characteristics. He no longer is immersed in mystery. Even interpretation is not speculative; interpretation of scripture, God's word, begins with what is there, in English, on the page, and the idea that God is not, in fact, American is a sacrilege. The rise of the US Christian right and the conflation of Christian values with American values may or may not be a religious fundamentalism, but it is a state fundamentalism – America right or wrong, but America blessed.[5]

THE LABOUR TOWARDS THE LUMINOUS

But there is a luminosity almost as a dissident and partially corrective force. All the religions of the Book have this force. In Judaism, Emmanuel Levinas, apart from his clear place in French philosophy, was a noted commentator on and interpreter of the Talmud.[6] But he insisted upon the reinsertion of spiritualism into Judaism[7] and on transcendence as having both a spiritual quality and a means of recognising and living with others.[8] Even the latter-day intellectual, Bernard-Henri Levy, has called for a luminous Judaism immersed all the same in world events outside of Israel alone.[9] The Sufis have always been a transcendent spiritual force in Islam, prefigured by the writings of great Persian poets such as Hafiz and Rumi.[10] And, in Christianity, the charismatic worship of many African churches and congregations reenact the launch of Christianity, where tongues of fire inflamed and inspired the frightened apostles fearing persecution after the execution of Christ (Acts 2:1–21).[11] As Paul Gifford has suggested, this directly counterpoints the efforts to export a more fundamental Christianity to Africa by recent American evangelists.[12]

The luminous has been a feature of Christian mystics for hundreds of years but, in the twentieth century, there have been notable examples of religious thinkers striving for luminosity, including in the United States – although parent churches have often frowned upon them. Three from the middle of the twentieth century deserve mention, two Catholic and one Protestant.

Born in France, but situated mainly in the United States – apart from some years in China – Pierre Teilhard de Chardin (1881–1955) was a highly trained palaeontologist, who studied evolution scientifically but also as an expression of humanity's relationship with God.[13] Not just developing in biological terms, humanity was evolving in mental and social terms towards a spiritual apotheosis, a unity with the Godhead, with what he called the Omega point – this term drawn from Christ's self-description in the last chapter of the last book in the Bible, the Revelation (22:13), 'I am the Alpha and Omega, the Beginning and the End', the Omega being the resolution of all progress and growth. All evolution ends at this resolution.

For Chardin, the critical point in human evolution was not so much biological as social. The moment of socialisation was the moment of community. The *Parousia*, the second coming of Christ, was not just a moment of Christ's arrival, but the arrival of that moment of development and evolution that allowed humanity's socialisation with the cosmic order.[14]

It was too much for literal-minded Christians, who had difficulty in any case with the scientific foundations of evolution, let alone its application to a cosmic resolution. After all, the Second Coming is imagined as heaven opening and a king riding in splendour on clouds, surrounded by angels with trumpets – not unlike aliens from outer space riding open-topped flying saucers. It was too much, also, for the Vatican, who suppressed publication of his great works. They appeared only after his death. The mystic nature of his writing seemed open to too many non-Christian influences and seemed also to elide established doctrine. Indeed, the idea of evolving towards a Godhead is almost identical to the teachings of the Hare Krishna movement, with its emphasis on the inner *atman*, loosely but insufficiently translated as 'soul', but pointing to a godly essence within that yearns for unity with cosmic godliness. It also seems to borrow from Hegel and the movement of history towards its apotheosis. But more difficult for doctrine was Chardin's sense that, in the evolution to cosmic socialisation, evil is only a series of growing pains. It is not a matter of a constant struggle between light and darkness as seemingly co-equal forces. It is not God verses Satan. Evil is only incidental in the path towards luminosity.[15]

Thomas Merton (1915–1968), like Chardin, was born in France but spent most of his vocational life as a monk in the United States. He died on a visit to Thailand. He has a revered reputation for his spiritual insights and for his devotion (although sometimes broken) to solitude. His autobiography, dealing with solitude and contemplation, has its own group of acolytes not always familiar with his other works.[16] Many of those other works were profoundly influenced by his studies in Eastern philosophy and mysticism. He conducted a correspondence with the Buddhist teacher, D. T. Suzuki[17] – who was learned in Pali and Sanskrit, and thus able to research the earliest forms of Buddhism in India.[18] Arnold Toynbee, the eminent British historian, also kept up a long correspondence with Suzuki.[19] And Carl Jung introduced one of Suzuki's works with a thirty-page appreciation and commentary.[20] I labour the Suzuki connection here as my view is that his Buddhism, of which he became an international influence, was not without its own influences from abroad, and its own association with the politics of his day. Suzuki was himself influenced by Bahai and theosophy, to which he was introduced by his American wife – he became briefly a theosophist – but his central belief was in a strand of the 'New Buddhism' of the 1800s onwards, as Japan made huge, determined strides towards scientific and industrial modernity, not to mention military modernity. The New Buddhism was an equally determined effort to ensure that there was cultural progress as well as scientific progress – not that Buddhism had to change so much as remain congruent with a new society with new instruments of social organisation. But this meant that Suzuki lent his prestige to the Japanese nationalisms that ransacked Asia and finally attacked the United States. And he approved of at least the early rise of Hitler and the expulsion of the Jews.

Merton, to his immense credit, did not subscribe to Suzuki's Buddhism, notably its Zen, in the way of an acolyte. He was himself too developed in his spiritual training to do that. But the idea of Zen, not as a religion, and not even necessarily as a Japanese practice, fascinated him. What he sought was a state of mind, an emptiness with an essential content of willingness to follow that emptiness.[21] The contemplation of that emptiness allowed the entry of the Grace of God. Following that line also led him towards Taoism.[22] The recent 2010 edition of his work on Taoism is introduced approvingly by the Dalai Lama,[23] whom Merton visited in India, where it is reported the two met as equals.[24] But the coherence of the concept and practice of emptiness in both Zen and Taoism – and Merton was fascinated, too, by cognate American Indian spiritual practices and appreciations – indicated to him a sense that one should, and perhaps could, not be bound by single religions. It was a view not popular with many in the Catholic establishment. That establishment view was bound by a more concrete, less abstract, sense of spiritual practice and certainly of religiosity. Given necessarily to a conservative, curatorial sense of Catholicism, and indeed on the other side of the divide also of Protestantism, it was nevertheless possible to break out of it as Reinhold Niebuhr, perhaps in a worldly manner, demonstrated.

By far the most 'American' of the three we discuss here, he also influenced other, non-theological, disciplines. The foundations of my own major discipline, international relations, was profoundly swayed by his concept of realism, an acceptance of *realpolitik*. Hans Morgenthau, the father of international relations realism, owed much to Niebuhr[25] who features in John Vasquez's classic compendium of the classics of international relations.[26] Niebuhr took the US side in the Cold War, but he was also a public intellectual of the left, being against the Vietnam War and remaining a sympathiser of the US working class. He became admired by a bipartisan series of senior politicians, including Presidents Obama and Carter, aspiring presidents like John McCain and statesmen like Dean Acheson. In a sense, this was because Niebuhr tried to have it both ways – a realist in world politics, he nevertheless advocated a Christian realism in which one had to balance right and wrong – but also the possible and the merely aspirational, coming down on the side of the possible.[27] In popular culture he is most remembered for the 'Serenity Prayer':

> God, grant me the serenity to accept the things I cannot change,
> courage to change the things I can,
> and wisdom to know the difference.

Making the right choice as to what is changeable – that is, not allowing a pragmatism to curtail, too soon, a difficult struggle – makes Christian realism a relativism. Martin Luther King admired Niebuhr and challenged the forces of darkness. Others, quoting this very prayer, or pious maxim, shrank away or made too cautious a judgement about what could be changed. There is no sense of martyrdom in this outlook – going to the stake for a conviction or a hopeless cause.

Nevertheless, there is a real theology that at least verges on the luminous in Niebuhr's work. His work has been identified with movements labelled as neo-orthodoxy and dialectical theology – referring to the interaction between states of sin and grace, love and justice, faith and reason. To an extent, it is impossible to reconcile these except by faith in God, and God – through the

Bible – has given a record of divine self-revelation. That self-revelation is to do with God's constant goodness. However, humanity's role in history has constantly been to corrupt what is good.[28] Human limitations on goodness stem from self-aggrandisement, meaning what Niebuhr referred to as a Promethean conceit –we think that we, by ourselves, can challenge the universe or, even without challenge, serve God individually and uniquely. This harks back to the Original Sin, which Niebuhr characterises as self-love.[29] By contrast, Christ's life and death was a revelation of sacrificial love for others.

Without that sense of outward-reaching community – that is, one loves God by loving others and by joining with others in communion with God – there can be no worship in a way that meaningfully reflects God's love to us and the sacrificial love of the Christ. Even a mighty nation-state that declares itself Christian needs to reach outwards and inwards.[30] It is the lack of love for others that led Niebuhr to condemn the Ku Klux Klan.[31] That would seem a simple enough condemnation to make, but he associated the Klan with Protestantism:

> It was Protestantism that gave birth to the Ku Klux Klan, one of the worst specific social phenomena which the religious pride and prejudice of peoples has ever developed. . . . I do not deny that all religions are periodically corrupted by bigotry. But I hit Protestant bigotry the hardest at this time because it happens to be our sin and there is no use repenting for other people's sins. Let us repent of our own. . . . We are admonished in Scripture to judge men by their fruits, not by their roots; and their fruits are their character, their deeds and accomplishments.[32]

As a Protestant pastor himself, Niebuhr was making a considerable statement. It is a judgement, however, that has also been made by others.[33] And it is a telling corroboration that almost all of today's New Christian Right, the institutional collectives of a fundamental – and indeed literal – Christianity in the United States is Protestant. It was the same with 'godly' endorsement of apartheid in South Africa. This is a condition requiring examination.

THE REDUCTIONISM OF GOD

It is one thing to think of God in neo-human terms. It is another to give God human prejudices. This is primarily present in the Old Testament, where God declares himself jealous and highly destructive. He has His enemies, not just in the spirit realm but on earth as well – even though no one on earth can actually challenge or attack Him. He is offended when His didactic sense of worshipful respect, which He is owed by right and by claim, is refused or

rendered imperfectly. As early as Genesis, He prefers blood and meat sacrifices as opposed to vegetarian ones (Genesis 4:3–4). And he does not like
humans talking in one language and building cities with tall towers. Rather
than seeing God as a tyrant – one who drowns people, burns them with fire
and brimstone, kills their children and throws them off their land – many
prefer to see this behaviour as exemplary and expressing a form of divine
licence.

In the biblical accounts, the people who die at God's hands 'deserve it'.
The inhabitants of the world before the flood were wicked – although it is
not specified what their wickedness consisted of. The citizens of Sodom
and Gomorrah were partly male homosexual, but there were sufficient other
attractions and amenities of the city for Lot's wife – clearly not a male homosexual – to feel compelled to turn back. All the firstborn children of Egypt
were slaughtered at the first Passover because of one man's intransigence.
And, as observed at the beginning of this book, Job's ten children were sac-
rificed as the result of a bet. The sense of proportion is what is lacking here.
So that as exemplary precedents they pose questions for those who act in
God's name as to who judges, who decides, who decrees the proportion of
blame, guilt, punishment and mercy? Although instances of mercy certainly
figure in the Old Testament, it is only in the New Testament Gospels that the
idea of mercy and forgiveness becomes centralised as doctrine. Even then,
in the Gospel of St Matthew and the Book of Revelation, holy slaughter is
prophesied.

If the New Testament is ambivalent as to whether it emphasises mercy or
damnation more, Jesus himself was emphatic that the old commandments
were now subsumed into two omni-commandments: to love God and to love
one's neighbours (Matthew 22:37–40). It is as if acting in God's name to
dispense righteous punishment and acting in Jesus's name to dispense love
are within a grand contradiction – perhaps a dialectical relationship of the sort
Niebuhr contemplated. It creates a grand tension in how to be a Christian,
and, indeed, those who favour an 'Old Testament approach' are somewhat
reinforced by the fussy almost rabbinic (he had been a rabbi after all) injunc-
tions and rulemaking of St Paul. This tension may be less able to be theologi-
cally expressed as presented in fiction, in a novel.

Morris West was, for fifteen years, a member of the Catholic religious
community the Christian Brothers, and this is reflected in his command of
theological debate and, above all, theological politics, which are presented
in his novels in a non-didactic way, seamlessly interwoven with his plotlines
and characterisations. Some of his characters are, in fact, quite recognisable.
In *The Clowns of God*,[34] Cardinal Ratzinger and the liberal theologian Hans
Kung are rather thinly disguised. The figure of the returned Jesus Christ is not.
But if this makes Christ and, to an extent, the other protagonists something

like cardboard cut-outs, the redeeming character is Pierre Duhamel – a jaded and elegant French politician who knows doomsday is approaching and still cares for his handicapped wife and the disabled children in his neighbourhood, the 'clowns of God', with a grace that belies the fact that he and his president are caught between those with their fingers on the nuclear buttons and the limit of their power to influence them.

The novel is set in the end-times. The United States and the Soviet Union are about to go to war. Mendelius, a liberal professor of theology, escapes with crippling injuries from an assassination attempt. The pope has a vision that all is lost, but the Curia dares not publish it for fear of causing panic but, above all, out of concern that the Catholic Church would relapse into a time of divine revelations that would undermine the institutional authority of the Vatican. The pope is effectively deemed mad and retired to monastic seclusion. But his visions continue. Finally, he is released and makes his way, via an unsuccessful attempt at a Pall Mall club to persuade the Whitehall Mandarins of the need for action, to a rural commune where the family of Mendelius has gathered together with the waifs, strays and child clowns of the world, to await and hopefully survive the nuclear holocaust to come. The therapist of the former pope – who appeared at his hospital bedside after he suffered a debilitating stroke while trying to persuade the Whitehall Mandarins – has also made it to the hills where the commune awaits the worst, where he reveals he is the Christ. The commune has been chosen, he says, to be one of the pockets of survival, but everything and everyone outside the chosen pockets will die in the war. The community is outraged. Not grateful. They plead with the Christ figure. And, whether West meant to do this or not, their pleading echoes, almost exactly, Abraham's pleading with God for the survival of Sodom and Gomorrah. Abraham pleads for mercy, he pleads for proportion. He pleads for the sake of those deemed wicked. It is, in some ways, the most moving passage in the Bible. Abraham begins asking God:

> Will you kill good and bad alike? Suppose you find fifty godly people there within the city – will you destroy it and not spare it for their sakes? That wouldn't be right. Surely you wouldn't do such a thing, to kill the godly with the wicked. Why, you would be treating godly and wicked exactly the same. Surely you wouldn't do that. Should not the judge of all the earth be fair?

Then Abraham bargains God down: if not destroy it for fifty, preserve the city for the sake of forty-five? Then forty? Then thirty? Then twenty? Finally, quivering and shaking, Abraham pleads for the cities if there are ten (Genesis 18:22–32). Abraham is pleading for proportion, but he is also instructing God. As if He were the most powerful infant in the universe. In *The Clowns of*

God, the commune does the same, until the Christ figure finally relents. The book pans to the Elysee Palace where Duhamel and the French president are awaiting the end and finally hear that it has been postponed. For they would not have been among the ten, despite Duhamel's immense, if jaded, charity and care for others.

The contrast here is between the darkness of mass destruction and the illumination of mercy. It is human beings who show Christ – who had pontificated that the mathematics of the universe demanded destruction – the immeasurable Way.

West presents a drama with Catholic protagonists, but his God of destruction is strangely Protestant. The entire birth and growth of Protestantism was due to corruption within the Catholic Church, and its monopolies over life and the affairs of state and society. It was also, in the Middle Ages and Renaissance – notwithstanding the luminous teachings of St Augustine in the 300s to 400s – due to the efforts of popes to reduce and confine God as an instrument of the Vatican in alliance with kings and emperors. This was at first a necessary *realpolitik* as Europe faced an Islamic expansionism from North Africa into what is now Spain. The Battle of Roncevaux Pass in 778, celebrated in the eleventh-century epic poem, *The Song of Roland*, was a great stand against Islamic armies able to gain ground all the same by Christian treacheries.[35] Roland dies valiantly, partly because of his pride in refusing to call for help against overwhelming odds. When, finally, the armies of King Charlemagne arrive, it is too late for Roland and his companion, Oliver. Charlemagne went on to become Emperor of the Holy Roman Empire in 800, and its very name spoke to its mission to defend both Europe and the Christian faith. By this stage, Islamic conquest and administration had already established themselves in Andalusia (from 711), and the beautiful palace, the Alhambra, remains as a legacy of the cultural refinement of the 'Moorish' kingdom, as do the mosques and other great buildings of the Caliphate of Cordoba which by the early tenth century had extended itself over most of Spain. Only much smaller kingdoms, such as Castile, held out as Christian in the north. It was from Castile that Rodrigo Diaz de Vivar, *El Cid* (1043–1099), led a Christian fightback, again celebrated in epic verse dating from 1140.[36] But, even as the 1961 Samuel Bronson film starring Charlton Heston makes clear, Diaz had to make alliances with Islamic kings who were themselves fearful of more fundamental hordes pouring in from North Africa, curiously (and prophetically) dressed exactly like ISIS (Islamic State of Iraq and Syria) fighters of today, with swords rather than guns.

But at the time of Diaz, Europe was also beginning to stir to the need for higher learning of its own. In the 900s, the royal library of the Caliphate of Cordoba had five hundred thousand volumes, more than any Christian library, and its university admitted Christian students as well as Islamic ones. In 1088, a guild of Christian students founded the University of Bologna. Other universities followed, notably Paris (1150, officialised in 1215) and Oxford (perhaps 1096, officialised 1167). The University of Paris was famous (or notorious) for its theological debates ('How many angels can dance on the head of a pin?') and legendary for the ill-fated romance between Abelard and Heloise (suggesting the presence of female students). But this meant it was only a matter of time before the church sought to impose and cement its control over this new form of social organisation – and did so at the end of the thirteenth century with the first system of accreditation, whereby universities had to secure the Papal Bull, the *ius ubique docendi*, for their masters degrees to be recognised. The monopolisation of recognition for all important forms of organisation was a feature of church involvement in society – but monopoly also led to corruption.

The scandal of the Borgia family, particularly in the fifteenth century, producing kings and popes and corrupting those they had not produced, 'owning' them, without ever thinking this was impious or made a mockery of the pope as God's apostle on earth, was the nadir of the Catholic Church, following hot on the heels of a schism, not in the faith but in the high reaches of the Church, when rival popes ruled in Avignon and Rome (1376–1417), with support from rival European powers. It is no wonder that the early university students were constantly insubordinate thorns-in-the-side of local bishops. And it is no wonder that a professor of theology, Martin Luther, had finally had enough. The Borgia-born Pope Alexander VI, pope from 1492 to 1503, had set new low standards for papal behaviour, particularly in his sexually libertine habits. The College of Cardinals was dominated by people who had gained their places by nepotism, family ties or wealth. Only a minority were churchmen. The Vatican had essentially become an instrument of state or, more accurately, the instrument that ruled states. But, if it controlled kingdoms, its monopoly of entrance to the kingdom of heaven began to be disputed. Martin Luther, who lived from 1483 to 1546, famously nailed his ninety-five theses to his city's church door in 1517. Basically, he said you cannot buy your way into heaven. Not the pope, not the pope's indulgences, not even good works could do that. Only God's grace could allow you in. At a stroke, he removed the authority, the privilege, and the ultimate monopoly of the Vatican. The Protestant Reformation had achieved its champion. It was not just the Church that was split – all of Europe was split as countries rushed to take sides. War engulfed Europe.

The most infamous and destructive of the wars was what came to be called the Thirty Years' War of 1618 to 1648. Even those countries not directly participating were militarised. The saga by Alexander Dumas, *The Three Musketeers*, is set in this period, where rival militias reflected a France wracked by tension as war raged nearby. The end of the war led to the Treaty of Westphalia of 1648, whereby today's Western secular state system was inaugurated. Religion was no more meant to be the demarcating criterion by which a nation was judged in terms of its rightness or wrongness, and states, agglomerating into larger units – 194 European states had been involved in Westphalia – were offered a system of recognitions and guarantees against arbitrary violence.[37] The war was still a strong memory in Europe; so much of the continent having been ruined by it that more than a century later, in 1795, Immanuel Kant was still writing of ways by which constitutionalised social and political norms could prevent war and bring perpetual peace.[38] This sat alongside his other great philosophical works in which he discoursed on universal morals and the universal law, or *recht*, by which all humanity was bound to a code of ethics.[39] His fellow Enlightenment philosopher, Hegel, also wrote on both a sweeping spirit of history, a *geist*, and on a communitarianism which helped develop today's views on social organisation, civil society, and its ostensibly 'settled norms'.[40] But what this meant was that philosophy, albeit with borrowings from theology – a spirit of history seemed drawn from God's Holy Ghost – had now replaced a somewhat discredited sense of religion and was proposing new forms of the immaculate, the *recht*, the governing force over humanity.

Even before the philosophers, as the Thirty Years' War was just beginning, the Pilgrim Fathers in 1620 had sailed from Plymouth to the 'new world' of America. Protestant, idealistic, and sick of the decay and *ennui* of Europe, they sailed away for a new beginning. They founded a frontier society in which what became known as 'Protestant ethics' of hard work, making do and confronting physical realities, became the frontier normal, tradition and something that demarcated manhood, adulthood and the new nation. They also had God on their side, a new species of the chosen – but chosen because, in their self-reliance, they didn't bother God much. They would worship and they would seek guidance, but they would accomplish what needed accomplishing by themselves. They would effectively 'problem-solve'. Conceptualisation was for the European philosophers. And it is as if, many years later, all luminous theology was still trying to catch up with the *geist* and the *recht* of the European Enlightenment, utilising Asian tools and scientific analogies as it did so – desperately trying to enlarge God again.

GOD BECOMES RICH

Protestantism turned to the Bible as an antidote to the overlay of Catholic tradition and ritual upon the Bible and its teachings. *Sola sciptura* was a guiding principle. As Bradford Littlejohn expresses it:

One might fairly argue that, if anything, the Bible has come to occupy a *more* and *more* central role in many expressions of Protestantism, particularly in the United States.

But although the Reformation had been built firmly upon the foundation of the Bible from the beginning, it is important to remember that the doctrine of Scripture was not itself the pearl of great price which the Reformers sought to recover—that was the glorious gospel of justification by grace through faith. The doctrine of Scripture was, so to speak, the strongbox for preserving that pearl of great price: since God had revealed the way of salvation clearly, fully, and sufficiently in Scripture, no human word could add conscience-binding doctrines or traditions that could serve as conditions of access to God. Faced with the tortured uncertainty of his standing before God, Luther had proclaimed the gospel of justification, as revealed in the Word of God, as a basis of new-found certainty, by which the believer could approach the throne of God with confidence in his favor.[41]

The deeper the adherence to the Bible, the more certain the faith. The problem here was looking at the Bible more and more literally as a means of relying on it more deeply. This is, in a very real way, understandable. Protestantism didn't have a history of intellectual exponents of doctrine like Thomas Aquinas. And the Bible itself did not seem to require intellectual exposition. The New Testament, apart from a teasing few verses introducing the Gospel of St John, and the spectacular scenes in the Book of Revelation, could be read like the Old. The two could be read as narratives faithful to reality as it had occurred. The Pauline letters are letters of instruction – they can certainly be taken as literal – and the Gospels are accounts of a life that had been real. The parables and teachings of Jesus were counter-posed in the Gospels with the teachings of the scribes and Pharisees who were, themselves, always seeking to entrap Jesus with intellectual questions. The Gospels and the Acts of the Apostles could be read in exactly the same way as the Books of Judges, Kings and Chronicles of the Old Testament. And, if the Book of Revelation appeared at first mysterious, it could always be rendered as prophesying, for example, a literal battle to the death in the Valley of Megiddo; a very human-looking angel will literally trample the grapes of wrath.

But, if literal, what is interesting at this point is how a literally interpreted New Testament injunction towards poverty, or, at least, not accumulating riches on earth, was transformed into a virtue of accumulation that moreover denied benefits to those unsuccessful at accumulation. Here we discuss the Protestant work ethic. This has been regarded as Calvinist in its origin.[42] Indeed, thirty-two of the 102 Pilgrim Fathers were members of The English separatist Church, a radical wing of the Puritans, and much given to Calvinism. Austerity and uncomplaining hard work were hallmarks of this creed. That much is clear. How this led to the expectation that hard work can, and should, lead to accumulation, and that this is not only divinely sanctioned but blessed, was the stuff of a famous work by Max Weber: *The Protestant Ethic and the Spirit of Capitalism.*[43] This appeared in 1905, although most references to it cite the 1920 revised edition. Weber points out that it was not just Calvinism alone at work here, but a range of Protestant religions. He cites a 1748 essay by one of the founding fathers of the United States, Benjamin Franklin. Its famous line is 'time is money', possibly the most famous line still used in business transactions today. But Weber points to the moral language used by Franklin. Wasting time essentially is a matter of murdering it and its profitability.

> Remember, that *time is money*. He that can earn ten shillings a day by his labor, and goes abroad, or sits idle, one half of that day, though he spends but sixpence during his diversion or idleness, ought not to reckon *that* the only expense; he has really spent, or rather thrown away, five shillings besides. . . . Remember, that money is the *prolific, generating nature*. Money can beget money, and its offspring can beget more, and so on. Five shillings turned is six, turned again is seven and threepence, and so on, till it becomes a hundred pounds. The more there is of it, the more it produces every turning, so that the profits rise quicker and quicker. He that kills a breeding-sow, destroys all her offspring to the thousandth generation. He that murders a crown, destroys all that it might have produced, even scores of pounds.[44]

This advice to a young trader was in fact a direct riff off Matthew 25:14–28 –especially verse 29, which is a moral injunction from Jesus, and verse 30, which speaks of punishment for a moral crime. The parable tells of a businessman who goes off on a trip and leaves behind amounts of money for his servants to invest. Some of the servants invest diligently and wisely and greet their employer on his return with news of how they multiplied his money. But one servant, fearful of risks and work, had merely hidden his portion of the money away. He had lost nothing but had added nothing. He is excoriated for his lack of business commitment and acumen and has his funds confiscated and distributed to those who had done well:

> The man who uses well what he is given will be given more, and he will have abundance. But from the man who is unfaithful, even what little responsibility he has will be taken from him. Throw this useless servant into the outer darkness: there shall be the weeping and gnashing of his teeth.

This parable has been applied literally in a modern context. The King James Version of the Bible says that the businessman left his servants sums of money calculated in terms of 'Talents'. Nicholas Leone has calculated the value of a Talent in New Testament times and says that, in modern terms, the sums involved would amount to millions of dollars. He then uses the parable as a business investment lesson.[45] The conflation of Christian morality and financial maximisation becomes overt.

For Weber, the Protestant work ethic, as an ethic and principle pertaining to capital accumulation – of capitalist practice and of the development of modern capitalism itself – had three key features:

- In the new Protestant religions, an individual was required to follow a secular vocation, a *beruf*, with as much zeal as possible. It was effectively a religious requirement, a compulsion. The result was a likely accumulation of money and resources.
- The new religions, not just Calvinism but other austere Protestant churches, forbade wasting this hard-earned money. Spending it on luxuries was a sin.
- Furthermore, donation of money to the poor was effectively encouraging beggary. The impoverished were so out of their laziness. They not only sought to burden others, particularly those who had worked hard but, having not worked hard themselves, they were offending God Himself.

If this was, in Weber's argument, the social foundation for the birth of modern capitalism, then the United States certainly became the world's most successful capitalist nation. Insofar as the Parable of the Talents, and Weber himself, spoke of material increase – that is, capital represented both in itself and in terms of what it could do – evidence of its capacity was material and tangible. There was literal evidence of having worked hard, even if not evidence of luxury – although the frowning upon the purchasing of luxuries has certainly changed. The point here is the encouragement of a mindset that works in terms of literalisms.

But the commitment to a work ethic and its corresponding disdain for the poor is at odds with what follows immediately upon the parable of the investment of Talents. The new parable starts immediately in the very next verse of Matthew 25 and is told from verses 31 to 46, where the penalty for *not* helping the poor is damnation. This is the Parable of the Sheep and the Goats. In the Gospel of St Matthew, it is Jesus's very last parable, his final teaching. On the occasion of the *Parousia*, the Second Coming, Jesus divides people into two categories for judgement. The 'sheep' are praised for their charity to him: feeding him when he was hungry, giving him drink when he was thirsty, giving him shelter when he was homeless, giving him clothes when he had none, giving him medical aid when he was sick and visiting him in prison when he was incarcerated. The sheep protest that they had never done those things for Jesus. His reply is, 'Insofar as you did these things to the least of my brethren, you did them to me'. He then criticises the 'goats' for not doing these things, and the goats protest that they had never refused any of these things to Jesus.

'Insofar as you did not do these things to the least of my brethren, you did not do them to me'. The goats are sent to eternal punishment.

THE CITY OF GOD AND THE POLITICAL
KINGDOMS OF MEN

If, however, God had been reduced to almost a human scale, becoming a patron-saint of human survival and prosperity, a mere demi-god of the labour of one's hands, He had also escaped the inexplicable heights of St Augustine's fifth-century proposal of a City of God that placed anything and everything humanity could do into a whiter shade of pale.[46] Augustine proposed almost a Christian application of Plato's idea of ideal form. Even so, the very metaphor of a city meant a metaphor based on human recognition of what a city is. God cannot escape the limited human efforts at abstraction any more than He can escape human commitment to the material and literal. Even so, a luminous city, not unlike the luminous city described in the last two chapters of the Book of Revelation, the last book in the Bible, could be cast as an extreme entity beyond human capacity to construct (or even comfortably inhabit). Revelation's city is made of transparent gold, jasper, sapphire, emerald, topaz, amethyst, pearls and other precious gleaming substances – 2,400 kilometres long and 2,400 kilometres wide (Revelation 21:16–22) – so God, who takes the place of streetlights, has built a city that refracts His glory. It is to the condition of this luminosity that thinkers like Chardin and Merton aspired in their depictions of spiritual grace.

If this makes the most elevated Catholic thought into a contradistinction with Protestant materialism and literalism, replacing it with at least metaphor if not actual luminosity, it is not as if Catholic history is free from sometimes abject political compromise to ensure position within the material political world. Albeit not in the same modality as the popes from the era of the Borgias, but somewhat greater in its possible elision of godliness, the silence of the Vatican as Hitler exterminated six million Jews is something that can be debated, and has been debated, fiercely. For some, silence screamed of complicity. For others, there is no evidence that Pope Pius XII knew about the details of the extermination. Here, however, the politics of knowledge and action, or inaction, point all the same to an acknowledged enmeshment with politics. What did he know or not know from the Vatican's high political relationships? It was simply an enmeshment of guilt or one of not innocence but non-guilt. The distinction can be Jesuitical.

The highly controversial 1963 play *The Deputy*, by Rolf Hochhuth, effectively accused Pius XII of knowing complicity in the extermination by his silence.[47] It was both well received as an explanation as to why there had in fact been a Vatican silence during the war and vigorously criticised on grounds of incorrect or manipulated source materials. Hannah Arendt, however, maintained that Pius XII almost certainly had the facts of what was happening at his disposal and that the only question was whether the Vatican would have acted had there been a different pope.[48] Many questions were raised by others, such as John Cornwall, about the tolerance of Pius XII to the rise of fascism.[49] Pius XII has, however, been defended in efforts to argue how delicately positioned was the Church, with the pope both not knowing the facts and seeking to keep the Church in a position of influence should the war start to come to an end and a need for its good offices in brokering or negotiating a peace should arise. John Conway points to the existence of a non-Nazi internal opposition to Hitler of which the pope was aware, sounding out the possibilities the Allies might negotiate with a non-Nazi German government.[50] But this, in itself, suggested Vatican knowledge of the intricacies of what was happening in German high places. It may be said that the jury is still out on Pius XII, but the sense of at least an ambivalence at that time on the part of the Vatican remains strong. This is about how it should have used its role in politics, not about whether it was involved in politics, or whether it was aware of politics as war ravaged Europe and other parts of the world.

The close identification, not so much of German fascism but, for instance, of Croatian fascism with the Catholic Church at this time was apparent to the Croatian historian Slavko Goldstein. His account of the roundup of Jews in his country takes up a huge tome that has been reprinted around the world.[51] And, as mentioned earlier, Goldstein, as a young Jewish teenager, took to the mountains to join Tito's partisans fighting against Germany and the German-supported, fascist puppet government.

In more recent times, the sharp division between the Vatican and the liberation theology of many Latin American Catholic priests who prefer to side with the poor is an indication of an official church seeking to maintain its alignments with governments in largely Catholic countries, despite governmental corruption and repressions of freedom. In this there is a direct parallel between Protestantism and its dismissal of the poor, and Vatican refusal to throw its weight behind its own ministers to the poor. This almost disdain for liberation theology continued despite the assassination of a senior Catholic figure, Archbishop Romero, in El Salvador in 1980. In a turn of fortunes, Romero was canonised in 2018, Pope Francis breaking with his more conservative predecessors – but at exactly the same time as the influence of the Church was waning in Latin America and elsewhere.[52]

What the Catholic Church does with its 'dissenting' priests and other figures is not enlightening. The Curia, traditionally conservative and far more so than Pope John and the current Pope Francis, has not fully done away with the doctrinal policing from the Inquisition. People are not burned alive anymore, but they can be sanctioned, defrocked, made known they are beyond a doctrinal pale. In *The Clowns of God*, Professor Mendelius is questioned by the hounds of God who then come for the novel's pope. But Mendelius is clearly modelled on the Catholic theologian Hans Kung, himself sanctioned by the hounds. Yet it is precisely a figure like Kung who opens the Church to the illumination of other thoughts and faiths. Even more than Merton, who was open to Buddhism, Taoism and American Indian spirituality, Kung's ecumenicalism is immense. His convening of a Parliament of the World's Religions was ambitious – getting agreement from so many faiths was an act of diplomacy and itself an act of faith. But, in the end, with quite a number of problems along the way – not so much in overall shared belief but in the wording of presentational and contextual detail – he was successful.

His work was paralleled by that of the InterAction Council convened by former German chancellor Helmut Schmidt. This council consisted in, apart from Schmidt, twenty former presidents and prime ministers, including of the United States (Carter), the UK (Callaghan), Australia (Fraser who was co-chair of the council), France (Giscard), the USSR (Gorbachev), Singapore (Lee Kwan Yew) and Zambia (Kaunda). Notwithstanding the constant observation as to why such distinguished people could not accomplish, while in office, what they subscribed to after their time in office, the accomplishment of gathering them together was astonishing. If the real question was to do with the exigencies of politics and political institutions militating against political ethics, the same question might be asked about the exigencies of church institutions and politics militating against fully luminous ethics that could be applied across faiths.

The two groups, Kung's and Schmidt's, released twin declarations on global ethics and global responsibilities. A man of immense culture, Yehudi Menuhin, wrote the preface.[53] The accomplishment was not so much in convening two such high-level and, perhaps, overly experienced groups – naïve and youthful aspiration and idealism were missing, but the worldly realism of both groups did remain discernibly anxious for a better world and a greater spirituality – but in the fact that the two declarations were congruent. Saving the world and saving the world's soul were twin ambitions. Politics, too, could be ecumenical, and faiths could transcend their politics.

But if all of this, no matter how noble, was in effect a treatment of God and man within their bodies politic – a distinct and almost concrete form of embodiment – what mission for the disembodiment of God and, in Christian faiths, the disembodiment of Christ (after two millennia of depictions of his body nailed to a cross), is possible in an age that has drawn back even from the cautious hopes of Schmidt and his council and, in the age of jihad, from the ambition of Kung and his parliament? The hounds of God are never far from resurfacing in the Curia of the Vatican, no matter how bold the sound-bites of the pope, and the new right in politics is surfacing with a vengeance, in the United States tied directly with a concretised, material, literal and excluding form of Christianity.

DISEMBODYING GOD FROM THE CHURCH

It may be that human imagination is both fecund and highly limited. It constantly and creatively imagines God, but always in the image of human-ity. Even the pluralistic spiritual universe of Hinduism seeks to depict the gods as more than human by the simple attribute of giving them more arms, more heads, more eyes – so they can see and do more than mere humans. In Christian Renaissance culture, Michelangelo's great Sistine Chapel ceiling painting depicts God creating Adam but is, in literal terms, the image of two human figures touching fingers. In his great sculpture, the executed body of Christ mourned by Mary, the *pieta*, is of the same artistry as his statue of David. Mary mourns a profound human death and David readies himself for great human heroism. There may be a limit to any attempt to disem-body Christ, let alone God, and talk of a full luminosity when we are still researching the physics of light. The more we research through science, the more likely we are to create a sophisticated and advanced (for now) rendi-tion of Hubbard's science fiction world where aliens replace angels and we have simply upscaled our efforts to embody those things we do not know – because, finally, perhaps we cannot know.

That is one thing, but institutional embodiments of faith and belief – lock-ing them into churches and limited doctrines, liturgies and ceremonies, no matter how old – is a different problem entirely. This is why Kung's grand, perhaps grandiose, ecumenicalism was so important.

Once, there were tales of St Francis making a trip to the Holy Land in 1219, not to worship, collect relics or accompany the crusades, but precisely to seek peace, by his mediation, between Islam and Christianity.[54] There are eighteenth-century accounts of Jesuits on the roof of the world, in Tibet – although the most famous of these, that of Ippolito Desideri, was itself a study in contradictions. He tried hard to accommodate himself to Tibetan mystical thought, albeit with a vision of the people's future conversion, and worked hard, in particular, to refute the central Tibetan Buddhist belief in reincarnation – but learned the language and sought in some ways to engage with the religious leaders and royal courts. He was never able, in seeking his accommodation with mystical thought, to come to terms with, let alone refute, the core notion – it has to be a notion, as it cannot be conceptualised – of nothingness.[55]

He was, however, able to note how the doctrine of reincarnation had its political uses by earlier Dalai Lamas to ensure they could secure unchallenged positions in society – proof of appropriate reincarnation was proof of political right – there being the same hard edge to professed luminosity as in any other religion.[56]

And with hard political edge comes not only a degree of leadership forwards but also backwards – forwards to attempted illumination or backwards to doctrine which is as replete with prohibitions as it may be with permissions to approach God but only through institutional means. It leaves us the condition of direction and doctrine rather than Niebuhr's condition of Christological sacrificial love, rather than Merton's efforts, perhaps a little more successful than Desideri's, in appreciating the emptiness of Buddhism; rather than Chardin's fully mystical apotheosis whereby what had been scientifically demonstrated evolution became an evolving into, a socialisation into, a merger with, and an assimilation by the cosmic universe. It is not a church or churches that are thus assimilated, and the body in any of its forms, imaginations and ascriptions would really not matter anymore.

Chapter 3

To Be Embodied or to Be Embalmed?

Given the problems the West has with Islam today, the very worst thing it could have done was, perhaps, defeat the Ottoman Empire in World War I. Depicted as antiquarian and somehow decadent, it was anything but. Indeed, one of the striking features of T. E. Lawrence's account of his desert war against the Ottomans was that every time he and his marauding guerrillas blew up an Ottoman railway track or cut telegraph lines, the very next day an armed contingent of Ottoman engineers would repair them. Lawrence was fighting an informal war, but his adversaries were very much within formal modernities.

But one of Lawrence's observations, as we shall see, opens a generalised window to the future. Stopping over to rest in the oasis town of Kasim, he no longer finds it restful:

> The Wahabis, followers of a fanatical Moslem heresy, had imposed their strict rules on easy and civilized Kasim. In Kasim there was but little coffee hospitality, much prayer and fasting, no tobacco, no artistic dalliance with women, no silk clothes, no gold or silver head-ropes or ornaments. Everything was forcibly pious or forcibly puritanical.[1]

If, unknown then to Lawrence, the 'fanatical Moslem heresy' of Wahhabism was to penetrate huge undercurrents of Saudi domestic life and international relations, penetrate the very Saudi Arabia he was fighting to create. The then-centre – not so much of Islamic religion but of Islamic urban culture and, I use the term deliberately, cosmopolitanism lay in Istanbul, at the heart of the Ottoman Empire. Its early name of Constantinople, named after Constantine, saw it as a Christian capital, but it took on other names over the years – one with the meaning, 'Refuge of the Universe', because of its reputation for

47

tolerance. Jews and Christians lived together, sometimes uneasily but by-and-large reasonably, in an Islamic city of great beauty and learning.[2]

But even in the then-underdeveloped region of what is now Saudi Arabia, Lawrence's opinion of Wahhabism was partial all the same. A long history of interaction which has lasted to this day has meant a tension at the heart of Saudi Arabia. Wahhabism forms a counterpoint to the show of modernity in Saudi Arabia, some would say a limit. It has projected its presence into modernity with violence and drama as we shall see in the Siege of Mecca in 1979. But that was a conflict engineered by aristocratic figures in feudal Saudi society. They were part of the 'establishment'. So what we see as Wahhabism today exists and interacts as an intimate tension, a contradiction, within a dialectical relationship that must be constantly arbitrated and without which Saudi society and governance would be very different.

It was the Ottoman Empire that rebuilt Jerusalem after its long years of laying in waste after its destruction by the Romans and, as noted earlier, it is the Ottoman city that witnesses today's Christian pilgrims imagining they are walking the streets of Jesus. Also, as noted earlier, Herzl, the Jewish thinker who fixed the idea of Zionism to a 'state', would have at first contemplated an autonomous protectorate within the Ottoman Empire. If that had happened, perhaps there might have been a greater sense of administered proportion and apportionment between Palestinian residents and Jewish migrants, with the process starting well before the Holocaust.

But the Ottoman Empire also had subordinated the Islamic caliphate of the medieval to early modern times to the state. The caliphate all the same attracted Islamic adherence from many parts of the world and occupied a place not unlike a powerful Church of England in the Anglophonic Protestant world. It was also a remarkably heterodox if not ecumenical Islam that was subsumed to the caliphate.[3] But it was a creature of the state and not the state itself. The same openness apparent in heterodox Islam applied, not always consistently, to debate and development of the sharia system of law. It was not as static or moribund as it seems now – fixed and irreproachable. In short, within the Ottoman Empire was the balance of forces that accompanies all modernity as it looks forwards, as its vocation, towards the future.

All the same, it also looked back to a glorious cultural history of poets and philosophers, its links with Persia and the Islamic intellectual renaissance, the 'golden age' of Islam, which reached its height from the tenth to thirteenth centuries.[4] By the time of its overthrow, the Ottoman Empire was the last place on earth with a curatorial sense of this enlightened past within Islam, couched within an increasingly modern functioning state.[5]

What emerged from the rebuilding of the rump of the Ottoman Empire as Turkey was a determination not just to rebuild what went before but to engage at the most dynamic level with the forms of scientific and technological modernities that then appeared to be bestriding the world – in secular contexts such as in the Soviet Union – by which the triumphant Western powers of World War I could be matched.[6] Ataturk's Young Turks spoke precisely to this technological, cutting edge ambition.[7] After World War II, the same ambition fired Nasser's Free Officers in Egypt and set alight the Arab world, and political parties embraced secularism as the new crucible for modernity and overthrew backwards-looking regimes that were seen as conflations of antique Islam and royalist corruptions and, above all, of flaccid weakness in the face of Western strength.[8] The question is whether regimes, if they had combined Islam and modernity more aggressively, would have been such attractive targets of internal overthrow.

ENTERING THE MODERN WORLD

The states that arose after finally and problematically casting off Western imperial rule, but not the borders between them that had been agreed in imperial trade-offs, had all manner of modern problems but also thought processes derived from the past of how a state should be safeguarded.[9] The association of modernisation with militarisation – safeguarding integrity and the possibility of progress by centrally planned discipline – was a feature alongside the association between modernisation and secularity. Religion that looked backwards could not have a place in the front rank of those seeking to go forwards.

But it was not as easy as that. Dragging something with centuries of anchor, and anchoring thought, forwards towards a vision of modernity was always a project replete with difficulties. And militarised rule could not by itself suborn faith to secular doctrines, nor could it in due course suborn international currents of thought on democracy and free expression from being key influences on younger generations. I do not wish here to enter the full-blown discussion of state, politics and faith in the Middle East but, rather, do wish to reiterate some points made by others in what are regarded as 'classic texts' on the subject, placing their views against some recent events and debates in the course of this chapter. The first and key point has been made by James Piscatori and that is, notwithstanding efforts of modernising regimes to do exactly this, it is impossible to view religion and politics as 'ideal categories and takes no real account of them as social phenomena'.[10] The Muslim Brotherhood in Egypt may be seen precisely as a social phenomenon that combined religion and politics in an inextricable opposition to the regime – even if, largely undetected outside Egypt, the Brotherhood itself was host to internal factions, some of which saw modernity and plurality as either pragmatically or inescapably inevitable.[11] Continuing to outlaw the Brotherhood meant that its overall conservative demeanour, restricted from wider debate, continued

to iterate the fault lines between faith and secularity that ran through adherence to nationalism within imperial borders that cut across larger confessional
unity; and the problems of plurality within a state with religious majoritari-
anism but all the same minority ethnic and confessional groups – Christians,
Jews – and the always prospective clash of laws, secular and strict religious,
on the question of rights and freedoms. If the state forbade political freedom,
why should faith not mirror that in religious intolerance?[12] In fact, had a state
like Egypt been open to debate it would have become clear that the idea of
the 'state' was new not only in modern post-Westphalian terms but in terms
of Islamic jurisprudence – that is, legal thought was not bound to the idea of
a state,[13] so that there was a possibility for thought on 'how to be a state' to
move forwards in debate between secular and religious quarters. The lack of
this debate has meant efforts to impose state theory on the Arab world from
the outside have been made without full cognisance of the tensions expressed
above.[14] It is a form of theoretical orientalism, perhaps – which should instead
invite 'intercultural' debate on the meaning of human rights, for example.[15]
And it should also invite a recognition that, just as religion and politics are
not 'ideal categories', the intersections of debate and interaction between
socioeconomic modernity and confessional ideology are in a constant state of
negotiation and, thus, trying to separate them into 'ideal categories', viewing
confessional ideology as retrograde and retarding and taming them by 'securitisation', only invites arbitrary distinctions and greater authoritarianism, and
itself retards the opening of ways forwards.[16] The richness and complexity,
above all the complex humanism, in interpretations of the Middle East and
Islam by figures such as Albert Hourani are something missed by both the
West and the East.[17]

In a way, what Arab secularity tried to do was not only build modern nationalisms but, briefly and idealistically, a secular equivalent in Pan-Arab Unity to
the idea of the *umma* or Islamic family that transcended borders.[18] The sense
of Pan-Arab Unity gained huge traction after what was perceived as Nasser's
successful stand against the British, French and Israelis at Suez in 1956 –
although that had as much to do with US diplomatic action in the United
Nations (UN) as any discernible Egyptian or Arab prowess – but, at last, there
was a perceived retreat of the West and its onsite acolytes.[19] Had Pan-Arab
Unity been successful, perhaps there might have been, in what would have
been a very large assemblage of nationalisms and ethnicities, a greater capacity for pluralism and deliberation and a clear place for religion in a benign
Vatican sense of being a carapace, though not a foundation in itself, of unity.
That unity, or at least larger territories, was what T. E. Lawrence fruitlessly
sought – betrayal of his dreams and promises probably drove him to madness[20]
– but, instead, the Middle East was carved into territories of compromise to
suit the sensibilities and strategic postures of Britain and France.[21]

Even so, since very much is known about Nasser and Pan-Arab Unity, it might be well to look briefly at the thought of the Ba'th, the political party that, in very different stylistic forms, sought to transform Syria and Iraq. There was at one stage great popular enthusiasm in Syria for Nasser's vision, but the Ba'th vision of Arab progress, while in many ways consonant with Nasser's, had unique characteristics. The Ba'th should be seen in slightly different contexts in the two countries, and the party went on to split into two separate national entities. Both countries had very long histories before the arrival of Islam. Iraq, as its antique predecessor Babylon, was at the front of all early civilisation and culture. The legends of Gilgamesh and Uta Napishtim, adapted by Ezra's scribes in the rebuilding of Israel, originated from Babylon. Abraham came out of a province of Babylon. The Syrians pointed to their own immense culture, however, not as an artefact but as something continuous. Damascus and Aleppo were the world's two longest continuously inhabited cities. Syria bore the mark of enforced and cultivated cosmopolitanisms. Alexander left his imprint in the Ptolymaic kingdoms; Syriac (a form of Aramaic) imprinted with Greek, was the language of Jesus; the Crusader kingdoms built great castles and left their genetic imprint in the not-infrequent blond Syrians of today. These were the same castles studied by T. E. Lawrence in his early incarnation as a young academic.[22] Because the Syrian world was more 'current' and cosmopolitan than the Iraqi one, Syrian Ba'th looked down upon Iraqi Ba'th as an insufficiently intellectual provincialism.

Having said that, there were characteristics in common, as well as programmatic affinities – and these were more important than ideologies, as such. There was a genuflection towards Arab unity within a clearly nationalist framework, but there was no ideology of the sort found in a communist party. In fact, the communists were outflanked and traduced by the Ba'th in both countries. The Ba'th was aspirational, as its name implies, 'renaissance', meaning the rising up again of the Arab people after long periods of imperial domination and moribund, decadent governments. It was socialist in the sense of the nationalisation of key sectors and services but did not shun private property and enterprise. It was not unlike, for example, the early British Labour Party, except for one critical and determining feature. It was not deeply interested in electoral power, neither in the state nor in local authorities, nor even in factory committees. It was prepared to storm its way to power, and military alliances were key. Samuel Finer, in his classic study of military coups, devotes space to the Syrian example involving the Ba'th.[23] Beginning as a movement in 1947 in Syria, exported by intellectuals to Iraq, its chequered history of manoeuvre, force and internal bloodletting finally saw its rise to power and its cementing by Bashar al-Assad (father of the current president) in Syria[24] and Saddam Hussein in Iraq.[25] Centrally planned discipline was the key programmatic methodology in both countries.

Insofar as the party was essentially an urban-based phenomenon, cities were radial points for centrally planned and directed government. The more cities, and the better-developed they were, the more effective government could be. Insofar as life outside the cities incorporated people of a cohesive ethnicity or related ethnicities, a form of uniformity or at least cohesiveness of policy could be applied to the country. In the case of Iraq, particularly with its Kurdish but also other group distinctions, this was always difficult.[26] There, the problem was not so much Arab unity as it was achieving discernible national unity. The nationalist project was never completed, and the internationalist project was essentially a dream. Moreover, Iraq had not tasted defeat at the hands of a vibrant, new and militarised Israel. Syria had, as had Egypt, and that in itself was a binding force and an impetus for modernisation in order to compete against a clearly identified external foe. The idea of an external foe was one that consolidated all efforts to modernise in the region, demoting what were seen as impeding forces such as religion – removing one or more obstacles to their rush forwards and that had been no help at all in the struggle against Israel and the imperial powers before it.

PROBLEMATIC ENTRY TO THE MODERN WORLD: RELIGION AND IRAN

It is ironic that Persia, who released the Jews from Babylonian captivity, should now be seen as the chief enemy of modern Israel. In many ways, although not acknowledged in the West with the emphasis it deserves, Persia was a determining empire of all things Western. Quite apart from its liberation of the Jews from Babylon, its legends claim an absorption of Alexander – who did not die young but became a scientific Persian king – and the debates between 'the thought of Alexander' and the early illuminatory thought of Islam was captured in a great poetic cycle of the twelfth century,[27] itself representative of the immense philosophical debates in the region of that time – in which neo-Aristotelian and neo-Platonic thought was curated and debated at a time when they had been deemed lost in Europe's 'Dark Ages'. When the Crusades stormed the Middle East, they brought back practices of hygienic medicine and surgery learned from the 'other side', as well as imported notions of chivalry towards women from the lands they sought to conquer. In Europe, debates on whether women were simply superior animals had far from receded, and the gallantry and courtliness towards women celebrated in the fourteenth-century poem, *Sir Gawain and the Green Knight*, would have been impossible without Middle Eastern and Persian influences.[28] But, even before then, in the time of Zoroastrianism, dominant in Persia well before Islam, there were legends of ecumenicalism and religious tolerance based on the appreciation of religious knowledge and its intersections with philosophical debates.[29] Some of this surfaces in the great eleventh-century epic poem, a Persian equivalent to the *Illiad* and *Odyssey* – only longer than both put together and more philosophically engaged – the *Shahnameh*, or *The Epic of the Kings*. There is one passage with the Roman Emperor Valerian, who like the emperors before him could not defeat Persia, being taken to meet a great Zoroastrian sage who discourses to him on the ethics and teachings of the religions of the world, from Buddhism to Hinduism and beyond. He closes with a disquisition from the teachings of Jesus to rebuke the imperialism of Rome:

> The Spirit of the Messiah bears witness to this. Do you not see what Jesus son of Mary said when he was revealing the secrets which had been hidden? He said, If someone takes your shirt, do not contend too fiercely with him, and if he smites you on the cheek so that your vision darkens because of the blow, do not put yourself into a rage nor let your face turn pale. Close your eyes to him and speak no harsh word. In your eating be content with the least morsel of food, and if you lack worldly possessions do not seek about after them. Overlook the evil things and pass meekly through this dark vale. But for you now lust has become dominant over wisdom and your hearts have gone astray from justice and honour. Your palaces soar up to Saturn and camels are needed to carry the keys to your treasure-houses. With the treasures you have arrayed many armies in resplendent proud armour. Everywhere you fight as aggressors, destroy the peace with your swords and turn the fields into pools of blood. The Messiah did not guide you along this path.[30]

Notwithstanding the temptation to transpose today's United States for yesterday's Rome, a temptation certainly too much for many commentators in Iran, what this passage illustrates is a religious cosmopolitanism that radiated outwards. Zoroastrian influences on Christianity, particularly through its descendant cult of Mithras to which front-line Roman soldiers were exposed, are thought to have included the virgin birth and the flight into Egypt – and certainly the profound question of the relationship equality of light and dark, or at least the equanimity with which one faces the other – light, in faith, finally winning.[31] Until then, light faces darkness in a state of equivalence, much as God faces Satan in the Book of Job.

But what this means is that, in the negotiations between Iran and the United States on things nuclear, the Iranians came not as archetypical Islamic Ayatollahs but as extremely proud people with a long and deep history that bestrode the world. Failure to understand this and see them only in 'Ayatollah mode' has meant an under-estimation of what is involved in terms of loss of face in any compromise too far.[32] And, even though Persia went into steep decline as a world power in the years after the intellectual charisma of the tenth to thirteenth centuries, its legend lingered long enough for Christopher Marlowe's great Elizabethan play *Tamburlaine the Great* to have its eponymous hero, while hacking his way through conquest after conquest, pause and reflect in front of his lieutenants on what his pinnacle of achievement might be (act 2, scene 5):

> Is it not brave to be a King, *Techelles?*
> *Usumcasane* and *Theridamas,*
> Is it not passing brave to be a King,
> And ride in triumph through *Persepolis?*
> To ride in triumph through Perseopolis –
> To equal the Kings of Persia.

But, if this informs a deep background to senses of self, the centuries of decline were often attributed, in part, to the backwards influence of religion. Iran had become the centre of Shi'a and thus also at odds with the majority-Sunni Islamic world, but with a conservative clergy who seemed not affronted by governmental lassitude, carelessness and corruption. It stood aside from modernity and any role in addressing its problems. As we shall see below in the case of Saudi Arabia, the encroachment of modernity was hastened by the discovery and value of oil in the twentieth century – which brought with it huge problems not only in terms of internal adjustments to modernity but also in the interventions of foreign interests and forces. In Iran this was seen most sharply in the fate of Prime Minister Mossadegh, who in 1953 was overthrown in a coup stage-managed by external powers. A moderate, reforming and modernising leader, he all the same sought to establish national control over Iran's petroleum industry, knowing it was the key to future prosperity and change. The coup was orchestrated by what is now British Petroleum and the US Central Intelligence Agency (CIA)[33] – a fact acknowledged by President Eisenhower.[34] As well as seeking to regain control over the Iranian petroleum sector, the United States was wary of communist influence in the region and, in particular, Iran.[35] The Soviet Union was, to the contrary, wary of Mossadegh as anti-communist.[36] No matter how mistaken, the chosen way forwards for the Western powers was to reinstall the monarchy and to ensure the shah was compliant with their economic and strategic outlooks for the region. In return, the United States invested heavily in the country and can claim some credit for the rapidity of its modernisation. This continued through several US administrations and the shah proved such a reliable and faithful ally that there was even some tolerance for his aspirations for Iran to become a nuclear power.[37] The idea of an Iranian bomb is anything but new.[38] The shah was an amazingly vain man, pageants were held in his honour in the illuminated ruins of Persepolis. On the one hand, he sought to benefit his people with the fruits of modernity and what became the highest standard of living and per capita income in the region; on the other, he crushed dissent ruthlessly and his secret police and their techniques of torture were legendary. Tiny, outlawed bands of Marxist guerrillas were summarily executed on capture. If the clergy had earlier stood aside from politics, they were now quiescent – with one notable exception. This was Ayatollah Khomeini, around whom some of the senior clergy, the *ulama*, or wise leaders, began to rally. But it was not only he who led the way towards change. Change became bruted as the 'Red Shi'a' associated with the scholar Ali Shari'ati. But the two men, without fully knowing it, became established as a symbiotic axis for rethinking Iran and remaking Iran, the first part for the better, the second not necessarily so.

Born in 1902, Ruhollah Khomeini's early education belied the reputation in which he was later immersed. As a theology student, he was also deeply concerned with poetry and philosophy, regarding Aristotle as the father of logic and being a passionate reader of the Sufi poets. He himself was a poet, although his work was largely published after his death. But, as a man entering his maturity and rising in the clerical ranks, it was the shah who radicalised him. Some of this was certainly owing to a clear conservatism on Khomeini's part. He was offended by the modernising 'White Revolution' launched by the shah in 1963, which gave electoral rights to women and privatised parts of the state sector. It also expanded educational provision. It all seemed a major secularisation of the Iranian public sphere, and Khomeini led the religious backlash. But where he garnered public support was with what he called the shah's 'capitulation law', giving US soldiers on Iranian soil diplomatic immunity. He also linked US domination of policy to Israeli interests. Even then it was becoming evident that there would be two poles of power in the region. This was before the devastating defeat of Egypt in 1967 and Egypt's partially successful military response of 1973, and finally the Sadat-led *rapprochement* with Israel – leaving the way clear for what Khomeini foresaw – that is, the prospect of a standoff between Iran and Israel, at best a balance of power between the two. Khomeini combined his critiques with stinging insults against the shah and was finally imprisoned and then exiled, first to Turkey and then to Iraq. He spent thirteen years in Iraq, leaving only in 1978 after Saddam Hussein personally explained to him that US pressure was becoming sufficiently intense enough that Iraq could no longer host him – but that he had arranged for the French to give him temporary residence in Paris.[39]

There were some ironies here. The more obvious is that not long after the success of the Iranian Revolution in 1979 which deposed the shah, it was US encouragement together with US and Saudi funding that prompted Saddam to wage a bitter war against Iran from 1980 to 1988.[40] The United States hoped Saddam, then regarded as a Western ally, could bring down what was already regarded as a dangerous regime; and the Saudis hoped for a diminution of Shi'a strength and its regional religious rivalry. Saddam later became the international public enemy number one in the eyes of the United States, and bitter war was waged against him and his secular and modernising, albeit ruthless, regime.[41] The first irony, of course, was that Iraq, of mixed Sunni and Shi'a populations, with the latter being the larger but with Saddam himself being Sunni, nevertheless hosted the exile of Khomeini with all courtesies, and it was Saddam who, in person, explained why Khomeini was required to move on. But when Khomeini reached Paris, he found he had been preceded by Ali Shari'ati, an Iranian thinker who had already amassed a reputation. Khomeini would have been aware of his work, but not its impact, especially upon young intellectuals in the Iranian diaspora, and the respectful reception it received in the French philosophical circles around Jean-Paul Sartre. Khomeini was also to learn the views and philosophies of other Middle Eastern diasporic groups in Paris and, in his own way, become exposed to the crosscurrents of thought for which Paris remains famous. Palestinian exiles, for instance, explained to him the work of Frantz Fanon and effectively gave him seminars in the *dependencia* critique of metropolitan accumulation through its domination of an internationally linked series of national class systems.[42]

Ali Shari'ati translated Fanon's great work, *The Wretched of the Earth*, into Farsi, so Khomeini would have been able to read it. Sartre, who wrote the preface to the book also wrote a preface to Shari'ati's work. Even an exile in Paris of only one year allowed Khomeini a cosmopolitan immersion. The Khomeini who returned to Iran for the revolution was, even so, the cleric who sought to sweep away the secularity of the shah and fell back on his earlier conservative visions of a pure Shi'a. The 'Red Shi'a' attributed to Shari'ati could not be ignored. It had to be incorporated as somehow the intellectual seed of the revolution, but the state that emerged was not given to the cosmopolitan society of Shari'ati's vision.

Even so, it could not be a state that only looked backwards. The antipathy of the United States required it to look externally as well, and the state, basically, also became a cause. 'Article 3, Section 16 of the Constitution of the Islamic Republic states that the Islamic government of Iran would engage all provisions to realise the formulation of a foreign policy based upon "Islamic criteria, brotherly commitment to all Moslems and unqualified protection of all the deprived of the world"'.[43] This last commitment to the deprived of the world is a clear echo of *dependencia* thought, where the deprived are not simply miserable as a 'found' state, they are miserable because they have been immiserated. And the revolutionary state could not avoid modernity. Its constitution, while seeking to express a state in Islamic terms, nevertheless, is studded with a succession of 'exceptional clauses', whereby issues not envisaged by foundational Islamic principles had, somehow, to be constitutionally expressed. Modern practices to do with, for example, medicine, states of political emergency and even contract law with modern means of exchange had to be constitutionally contextualised – meaning that sharia is secondary to the constitution, and the theocratic state has become essentially what Schirazi calls a hierocracy, a government dominated by clerics[44] – albeit with so many checks and balances to ensure no single institution of government, and no faction of clerics, can easily checkmate another that it is amazing that government works at all. This has required of course the emergence of a supreme ayatollah who superintends, balances, chooses among the ways forwards. Khomeini was that by default, as leader of the revolution, but his successors are that by necessity as much as anything else, power plays included. But it means, depending on the ascendant faction of the moment, some reformative modernity is possible. The question is that if the United States had not continued its hostility towards Iran, and it has been unremitting, would government, as a whole, have loosened towards greater such modernity. Under a state of siege, the cause is not just an Islamic solidarity in the world but survival. But this US siege of the country does point to Fanon's diagnosis of the world inflected in Shari'ati's work.

The Iranian Revolution featured a brief 'Tehran Spring' of amazing cultural production, before the revolution's capture by the clerical faction led by Khomeini.[45] This was what Foucault was referring to (in what has since been designated as his amazing naïvety and lack of judgement) in 1979 when he described it as a revolution of the spirit which had transformed the subjectivity of an entire people.[46] To be fair, at that stage no one knew how the revolution would degenerate from a people's subjectivity, to an attempted theocracy to an effective hierocracy that, all the same, encompassed national solidarity in the face of US siege. But it was to that subjectivity of a people, to its background culture and modernistic aspirations, to its sense of history and proud independence that Shari'ati addressed his writings.

For a long time, Shari'ati and his work was little known in the West. Ali Rahnema's sympathetic intellectual biography helped changed that.[47] And there are now repositories of his work online, translated into English,[48] as well as extensive bibliographies of work related to him.[49] The most popular (and most downloaded) of his works is *Fatima is Fatima*, widely regarded as a feminist invocation, using the daughter of the Prophet, who accompanied the male warriors to war, as a role model. Its actual feminism by today's widespread standards is far from fully expansive, but in the context of restrictions on women in today's Iran, it remains a signal for freedoms not currently available. But this does mean that, in a world context, some of Shari'ati's writing is dated. What he brought to the world's intellectual table, however, was a methodology of thought that combined, not always easily, spiritual and philosophical thought. Educated in Paris to the doctoral level, he was exposed to French philosophy and moved in philosophical circles. At the same time, he was anxious to compose an intellectual agenda for freedom in Iran that began with a freedom to think both authentically about Iran and knowingly about the outside world. It was not just a syncretic project but one in which he sought to make different styles and objectives of thought organically whole. It was magnificently ambitious – hence Rahnema's description of him as a utopian – but it was nationally purposeful.

Part of this methodology utilised exactly the poets that the young Khomeini admired – including Rumi and Hafiz – but it was also imbued with the Marxism of Sartre's later Hegelian moment, repudiating materialism as a sole basis of revolution and insisting on a 'spirit' in history;[50] and the humanism Sartre insisted on was part of existentialism.[51] It echoed Fanon's sense of an unequal world, but this world could be equalised all the same by an equivalence in thought. This thought had to relate to the world of Shi'a, thus the label attached to it by others, 'Red Shi'a'; but this relationship could only be achieved if the Iranian clergy reformed their approach to modernity and, above all, reformed their sense of organisation and purpose of organisation. Shari'ati looked first to the Catholic Church before settling on the Church of England as a model organisation – attached to but not determining the state, with a synod that had lay representation alongside the bishops, or, in the case of Iran, the ulama. How far Shari'ati was prepared to press this last point is unclear, but the Church of England as a reformative model was certainly there. Only a reorganised church could lead the way to stand against the shah and his increasing repressions. The theology of it all lay in Shari'ati's concept of longing. He invented a fictional heroine, Solange, who had drowned in the English Channel, and Shari'ati's longing for her became a metaphor of the worshipper's longing for God. This was fully Sufi in the sense of recognising the possibility of a personal relationship with God not necessarily mediated by the church, but this also accorded, by inference, a degree of freedom to each individual. To make thought drawn from secular sources cohere with thought that was spiritual, Shari'ati used the poets and their technique of illuminating metaphor that, at a stroke, carried a logic forwards by intuitive means.[52] Shari'ati's was not Western philosophy in any analytical or rationally logical sense. It was in its own way a leap of faith into the future. It accorded far more with the Tehran Spring than with the arid rule of the clerics that suppressed that brief moment of free cultural expressionism. Shari'ati wrote as if one of the great thirteenth-century thinkers of the Middle East at its crossroads with Persia, transported into and accommodating himself with the inescapable needs of the twentieth century, including the need for freedom.[53]

Of course, Iran did not follow this path. The clergy did reorganise itself and, albeit with factions – some of which could be described as more moderate and 'socially modern' than others – became, essentially, a suppressive national institution. Iran did follow the path of technological modernity of the shah – and indeed of Mossadegh before him – to the extent that its nuclear programme raised US and Israeli fears that the Iranian ambition was moving towards nuclear armament. It probably was, and the entire John Kerry set of negotiations was to slow it down for at least ten years. Along the way, he learned what a sophisticated set of men would sit across the table from him. So, exceptional people and exceptional accomplishments are possible, almost as an emulation of exceptional clauses in the constitution. Whether exceptionalism will take Iran forwards into a more liberal future mirrors the question asked also about its antagonist and US ally, Saudi Arabia.

PROBLEMATIC ENTRY TO THE MODERN WORLD: RELIGION AND SAUDI ARABIA

Perhaps the Saudi case is more problematic and complex than that of Iran – though perhaps not as thoughtful. Even Henry Kissinger in his late-career writings and reflections saw Saudi Arabia as playing a double game[54] – a respectable Westphalian state on the surface and the covert instigator and funder of many of the world's problems under the surface, reflecting a religious fundamentalism less sophisticated than Iran's but more influential in world affairs.

Saudi Arabia emerged into independence from Ottoman rule after World War I, smaller in size than T. E. Lawrence had hoped, although the tribal chieftains he had served did emerge as the royal family of the new and impoverished state. No one thought the country of great importance and, above all, of great capacity – it was a kingdom of endless sand. It hosted the holy cities of Islam but had no wherewithal to direct the course of Islam. And it had emerged with a history of tumult, blood, betrayal and the accommodation of what Lawrence observed in Kasim, a Spartan, puritanical, starkly desert-born Wahhabism. That history was bloody, internecine and a cohabitation (that often bloodily fell apart) between a feudal idea of the state and a wilderness-born ascetic idea of the faith.

It had begun well before Lawrence set foot in the Middle East. Although part of the Ottoman Empire, it was not always worth the empire's effort to keep it under control. So insurrections and factional conquests were part of the history of the area, but none of them fully dislodged Ottoman rule. The Ottomans waited, then came back with more modern force than the tribal insurgents could muster. What Lawrence brought to the equation, and this is not often recognised, was a militarily strategic brain – and a touch of complete madness, as in his attack, crossing the desert, on Aqaba – where the Ottoman forces, convinced a sizeable military force could not cross the inhospitable desert to attack them from the rear, had all their heavy guns pointing seawards in expectation of a naval assault.

But before this time, in 1744, the House of Saud made an alliance that changed the history of the region in a way that has lasted to this day. The alliance was with the forces of the preacher, Muhammad ibn Abd-al Wahhab. The armies of Wahhab and Muhammad ibn Saud combined, and a Saudi state was proclaimed in Riyadh. The Ottomans retook the city in 1818. By 1841 the House of Saud had been driven to Kuwait. But in 1902, the forces of the two houses came together again and regained some of their former territory. After World War I, with the defeat of the Ottomans, the Saudi forces were able to concentrate upon the defeat of the sharif of Mecca, who had been the formal point of cooperation with the British during the war and seized control of the holy city. With that in their grasp, they began to turn upon their Wahhabi allies, slaughtering the main Wahhabi army in 1929. That was the prelude to the independence of what we now know as Saudi Arabia in 1932. It was dirt poor – desert-sand poor – the fifth poorest country in the world, until the discovery of oil in 1938. The desert did not turn green, but the cities became opulent.[55]

That opulence, the capacity for which was dramatically increased after the petroleum price wars of 1973, a global struggle won decisively by the Arab oil-producing states, became too much to bear for the still-simmering adherence to the doctrines of the Wahhab within both the population at large and in high places. That doctrine was a pristine and stark vision of life as Muhammad had lived it – neglecting to acknowledge that he was a prince. But the idea was that the desert was itself a metaphor for the simplicity and honesty that God intended for human life as a whole – uncontaminated, including the lack of contamination by the presence of foreign non-believers.[56] It was (and I say this advisedly since Wahhabism has attracted much often-merited bad press) an Islamic form of Christological thought – not what the opulent Vatican thinks is Christian faith, with its overlays of splendour while preaching Christ's poverty, but actually living that poverty in, for instance, the style of the Franciscans. There were never, however, Franciscan armies that imposed that Christological ideal, although some would detect in Protestantism a coerciveness, especially in the Puritan leverage within the English Revolution. The Puritan analogy can be overdrawn, but the sense of reaction at least against over-opulence and infidels on holy soil caused much carefully but barely concealed concern and resentment in Saudi society. And it must be stressed that, within Islam as a whole and the various schools of Sunni, there have long been concerns about issues that have been very largely condensed upon Wahhabism,[57] and upon Wahhab's own supposed inspiration, Ibn Taymiyyah, who lived in the late 1200s and early 1300s – but who was a man of far greater complexity and variability than his popular appropriations today.[58] If not Wahhab himself, his own legacy is, as we shall see, more complex than many reductionisms allow. But it is fair to say that one part of his legacy was the animation behind what has become known as the Siege of Mecca in 1979.

Finally, as a point of disgust with the contamination of Islamic life, the siege was a carefully planned insurrection led by figures from Saudi high families. It was superbly militarily planned and fully researched beforehand. From the start, there has been nothing simplistic about the application of force in the cause of Wahhab. On 20 November 1979, Juhayman al-Otaybi led five hundred insurgents in a seizure of the Grand Mosque, the holiest of Islamic shrines, when thousands of pilgrims were present. The BBC captured – from a distance – some of the battle that ensued.[59] Scores of films and documentaries followed. Yaroslav Trofimov wrote an in-depth book,[60] which he defended in extended interviews.[61] The defence was due to the controversial nature of his analysis – not so much of what happened in the battle but of what happened afterwards.

The insurgents held the worshippers as hostages, took up sniping positions in all the minarets and entrenched themselves in the maze of underground tunnels – of which they had acquired detailed plans. Arms and explosives had already been smuggled into those tunnels. Otaybi's ancestors had ridden with Ibn Saud as he and Wahhab stormed out of the desert. He named his brother-in-law the new *mahdi*, the 'messianic redeemer', and others in both his family and among the insurgents had parents who had ridden with the Wahhabist army when it was defeated in 1929. It was a moment to restore the purity of Islam, certainly, but it was also a moment of revenge.

Wave after wave of Saudi military assault failed to dislodge the insurgents. At one stage, ten thousand Saudi soldiers were involved – to no avail. Finally, it was foreign forces who turned the day, but accounts, and legends, are divided as to who did what and by what means. Dropping bombs into the tunnels through ventilation shafts killed as many hostages as insurgents. Pumping gas into them may or may not have worked. Even more uncertain is what foreign forces or the combination of foreign forces were involved. Perhaps the CIA. Perhaps French elite forces who ceremonially converted to Islam so as not to defile the holy place before they commenced their assault. The current best guess is Pakistani commandos, and there is even the urban legend and boast that the later–military dictator of Pakistan, Pervez Musharraf, led the attack.[62] But, whoever had recaptured the Grand Mosque, great damage was done to people and reputation. The siege had lasted two weeks, and Saudi forces could accomplish nothing. The death toll came to 255 people, with 560 injured, and although most of the insurgents were captured, some escaped. Sixty-seven captured rebels were beheaded in various cities as a public display and warning. But this did not deter the clear impression that the House of Saud had failed to safeguard the holiest of holy places. Far from being the defeat of insurgents inspired by Wahhab, it gave the Saudi clergy, with clear Wahhabist sympathies, clear leverage to shape the Saudi Arabia of the future, both domestically and in terms of its foreign policy. They became the shadow state within the state. What emerged from the Trofimov account is what may be regarded as the grand treachery in today's international relations.

In return for continued support of the House of Saud, the clergy demanded and received a determining role in social policy. This had a direct influence on education. When ISIS (Islamic State of Iraq and Syria) later conquered Mosul and established its administration there, Saudi textbooks were regarded as perfectly suited for their own educational curriculum.[63] The continuing obstruction of rights for women owes to this clerical determination. In foreign policy, however, Saudi Arabia was to continue to all intents and purposes to act as a Westphalian state and not to sever its ties with the United States. However, it was to turn a blind eye to 'non-state' financing of jihad abroad. All Osama Bin Laden did was be a visible actor in what was meant to be a huge shadow enterprise. But, as with Osama, it began in Afghanistan and involved cooperation not so much with another state but with an agency of state – itself a shadow state – and that was with Pakistan's Inter-Services Intelligence (ISI). It may be said that it was an unusual, if not unique, twentieth century axis of two shadow states – except that both adroitly used their parent states in channelling huge financial flows from both Saudi Arabia and the United States. In the first instance, such channelling was most apparent in the joint Saudi–US financing of Saddam's war against Iran in the 1980s. The Saudis alone put in $30.9 billion (although this figure, though commonly cited, is unverifiable). However, in the early stages of the war against the Soviet occupation of Afghanistan, it is estimated that the Saudi government's financial assistance of the mujahedeen resistance was $40 billion, alongside private Saudi contributions that were also in the region of billions.[64] Both public and private funds, as well as the covert but massive US funds, were funnelled into Afghanistan by the ISI of Pakistan.[65]

These experiences led to expertise in covertly financing jihadist groups, to equip and sustain them – not to mention to keep their doctrinal morale high. The sudden appearance of huge fleets of Toyota HiLux pickups in Iraq under ISIS flags, with armaments all mounted in the same way, reflects considerable central planning. The Taliban had assaulted Kabul with such vehicles, so battle doctrine had a long gestation – but it worked, as expensively US-trained and equipped Iraqi regiments, one after the other, collapsed before the mobile ISIS storm. But Afghanistan was not only a case of learning how to do it but also a reflection of the division within the clerical vision inside Saudi Arabia. With knowledge of the United States, and full cooperation with it, the Saudi $40 billion financed the mujahedeen resistance to the Soviet occupation. It could be said that it was to help the oppressed but heroic members of the Islamic family. But very many of the mujahedeen warlords were perfidious and oppressive in their own right – hence the rise of the Taliban as an idealistic force to oppose their oppression.[66] Osama, who had personally fought with the mujahedeen, turned upon them by siding with the Taliban, helped finance them from his own family fortune, and earned the wrath of the United States, and at US behest the wrath of Saudi Arabia. Fighting against the infidel Soviet Union was one thing; fighting against the infidel United States was a greater thing, the United States being far more intrusive upon the lands of the believers than the Soviets, intrusive even into the deep reaches of Saudi Arabia itself. The question is whether, in the deep recesses of the Saudi shadow state, there are the seeds of its own downfall, curiously in the name of Islam.

But this may be why Saudi Arabia continues, under the terms agreed after the Siege of Mecca, to turn a blind eye to its nationals acting to finance and help direct ISIS – something surely captured by US intelligence agencies – for it buys off the radicals in the very shadow state which Saudi Arabia hopes will not turn, once again, against the formal Saudi state.

THE EMBALMED BODY AND THE PROBLEMATIC MODERN WORLD

If modern 'Islamic fundamentalism' was born not just of religion but of religion acting through a state, then the question of how to deal with it is certainly doctrinal but also hugely political. The secular revolutions of Ataturk, Nasser, even Assad and Saddam, as well as Ghaddafi, had in mind the breaking of the symbiosis between religion and state and prioritising the state as a modern provider – albeit in every case with centralising strongman tendencies and methodologies. In both Saudi Arabia and Iran, the symbiosis has returned, with a clear religious dominance of the relationship in Iran and a pretence that it does not in Saudi Arabia. But what does the 'pure' and 'purified' state seek? It seeks outside itself. It seeks a purification of the international state system, or a quarantine of one from the other. Never has the idea of the *umma* been more the unspoken agenda – with the problem of, as with Serb communities in Bosnia and Kosovo, what to do with Islamic communities in the West, of what incorporation into a trans-state *umma* with macro-state attributes, particularly binding law, is possible? No other problem in today's international relations poses such a problem of state fragmentation with adherence to a body of thought, norms, practice and laws outside the host state. But what is this fundamentalism – especially when it strikes against the 'forbidden'? Here, the Islamic world is itself embroiled in debate.

However, a differentiation needs to be reinforced. Outside its surrounding region, Iran has not been involved in active international terrorism. Former UN assistant secretary-general, Giandomenico Picco, who, in the 1980s, negotiated the release of hostages in the Lebanon held by Iranian-supported groups – by the simple expedient of allowing himself to be kidnapped four times by these groups so he could get a fast track to negotiations with their leaders – stressed the regional nature of this terrorism, and noted it was not more widely and internationally spread.[67] There were two good reasons for this. The first was the terrible cost and damage of the Iran–Iraq war then in progress, with Iraqi forces clearly supported and financed by the United States and Saudi Arabia. The temptation to lash back against the United States was tempered by the need to conserve strength and avoid further retaliation. The second was simply a question of propagating such regional hegemony as was possible for Iran – that is, among Shi'a populations. There simply is not the huge international hinterland of Shi'a affiliation that in any way begins to rival that of Sunni persuasion. And, in simple but critical terms such as visa access, Saudi operatives could be far more easily planted in the United States, ready to detonate 9/11, than anything comparable for Iranian personnel. This is not at all to diminish the acute sense of rivalry and sectarian animosity felt by Saudi Arabia towards Iran, nor to demean the sense of threat Israel perceives from what could become an equal opponent. Even so, at the very least there have been no Iranian-supported attacks on particularly US targets, whereas someone like Osama Bin Laden, and many others, clearly indicated a bellicose antipathy towards the United States.

Because of this, we shall here contemplate mainly the debates within Sunni political communities and involving thinkers who are themselves Sunni, on how far the values and community of Islam can be propagated abroad and, tellingly, as the world condenses in its communications and immediate contest of values via electronic media and constant air travel, what the homelands of Islam should or could do with currents of thought considered at one time as forbidden but now entering their societies.

For Tariq Ramadan, an elegant thinker of some openness, but often a controversial one all the same, the question of accommodation in Europe works both ways. Islam must certainly become more European – but Europe must also allow itself to become more Islamic.[68] The problem of this formulation, if it is not to be just a social desirability, is that Ramadan does not touch upon the logistics and wherewithals of this accommodation. Who legislates for whom, and how? Through which institutions of what democratic base? There were places like Istanbul and the university cities of Andalusia, and these were multicultural – but under ultimate Islamic rule. How to be ruled, by which laws and how, and what kinds of democracy to be legislated by are key.

The other closely related question is, Why just more Islamic? There are, in the United Kingdom, huge Hindu communities. The vexed question in India itself is how to better integrate stubbornly separated and opposed groups of Hindus and Muslims. Can Islam become more Hindu? Can Britain become both more Hindu and Islamic at the same time without turning 'integration' into a buffet dinner? And what of Caribbean cultures, Turkish cultures and Algerian cultures – the latter two, as Germany and France have discovered, have far more to them than just Islam. At some near point, a sense of grating could start to occur, and it may be simply in matters of taste and not even faith. I joked with Ramadan once as to what he found difficult in raising a teenage daughter: 'Her love of chemical hip hop'. But the long patience of any father can be at odds with those of shorter tolerance, who would ban all that seems out of the narrow reach of how cultures and, through them, faiths can be defined in reductive exercises. And Europe itself has great problems accommodating its long-established selves – the terrible wars in the former Yugoslavia being recent examples and in which, in the bloody and protracted siege of Sarajevo, a multicultural and multi-confessional city was shelled to rubble.[69] Its Europeanised Islam was the full frontal target of attack by those who thought they were more European and holy.[70]

The debate within the cities of the Middle East is precisely to do with what is holy and what is forbidden – devolving often to a 'pragmatism' as to who is *more* holy and to what *degree* something is forbidden. This is not to unduly simplify complex pathways and trajectories of thought but, rather, to provide an entry point to understand the thought of the Egyptian scholar and cleric Yusuf al-Qaradawi, who lived in Qatar for fear of his safety in the renewed militarised rule of Egypt until his death in 2022. He was also banned entry to the United Kingdom, and this is precisely goes against the 'pragmatism' and the hope that it raises for, if not Ramadan's unspecified mutual accommodation, some form of *rapprochement* on clearly understood grounds of value.

Having said that, Qaradawi is highly controversial. He sanctioned suicide bombers in Israel. But he also issued a fatwa sanctioning the assassination of Libya's Ghaddafi – on the grounds of, not of his secularism, but his own ruthless disregard for human life. This meant he supported the US-led NATO (North Atlantic Treaty Organisation) assault on Libya. It is difficult to isolate him in the 'box' called extremist or fundamentalist. The author of some 120 books, some far from short, he was most noted for his multivolume work on philanthropy as a requisite for a pious Muslim.[71] However, because many of his works did indeed deal with radical themes, his very history and standing as a 'dangerous' thinker has made his inclinations towards accommodation of new social practices more 'credible' to 'fundamentalists'. These inclinations may have been inching more towards tolerance than full-scale movements, and they were certainly not endorsements as such – but he had become more tolerant of even alcohol; he had moved against wife beating, rape and female genital mutilation, and inched towards female equality. There was not much inching, although perhaps some fractional inching, towards an acceptance of homosexuality. In short, he had become a little more 'modern', without seeing such things as a basic undermining of Islam. But it was on the question of violent jihad that he had been startling, proposing a series of theological tests that almost no atrocious jihad of modern times could pass. Where this is of the greatest importance lies in our recognition that today's large-scale, war-like jihad is exceptionally modern – in its computer hacking, weaponry, battle equipment, financing, battle doctrine, electronic communication, media presentation and global coordination.[72] In short, it is modern in its methodology. What is both not modern and not properly theological is its reasoning. It is here that Qaradawi, at the very least, proposed a debate, and in fact advanced an undermining of the theological planks of jihad's central doctrine. His thought on this is contained in a landmark book, *Fiqh al-Jihad* (2009),[73] which has attracted helpful explication, interpretation and commentary in English.[74]

Basically, in a lengthy work, Qaradawi takes on those who justify militant and military jihad because of what are called the 'sword *sura*', those verses of the Qur'an that call for the extermination of the infidel. These form the basis of the fire-and-brimstone sermons of radical preachers. In very condensed summary, Qaradawi's argument proceeds as outlined below.

1. There are far too many *sura* of peace and forbearance that require abrogation by the sword *sura*. Some scholars enumerate almost two hundred such *sura* of peace. They cannot all be abrogated in one broad sweep.
2. Not only that, but they also cannot be abrogated without dispute. If dispute remains, or is a dominant characteristic, then the sword *sura* cannot be absolute. It is not apodictic.
3. The sword *sura* and those like it are all contained within historical contexts which are not transferable.
4. There is the question of exigency – that is, the sword *sura* requires too much of the Islamic population; it demands permanent hostility to those who are not Islamic.
5. Thus, the sword *sura* cannot serve the purposes of a peaceful world, coexistence or humane interaction of a cosmopolitan sort.
6. Finally, the accumulated weight of Islamic scholarship over several hundred years speaks for the claims of peaceful relations in the first instance over those of jihad.

The word 'apoditic' is key here – established clearly beyond dispute. This does in fact invite dispute, but it is here where Qaradawi applies the weight of historical context and the overwhelming number of *sura* that seek tolerance and peace. If there is no offence, there can be no recourse to war. This, however, is where the matter elides theology and moves into the political realm – so that mistakes in Western foreign policy are taken as offence and these justify jihad not only on the grounds of defence but also on the inflected grounds of revenge. So there are two elements in seeking to prevent militarised jihad and its associated atrocity and war: firstly, the avoidance of foreign policy mistakes is uppermost (wandering gratuitously into theatres like Iraq unleashed maelstroms) the West can (slowly) learn to do that; but, secondly, there has to be engagement in theological reasoning and dispute – and the West is hopeless at that. The militant preachers have the field to themselves.

There is a third element, not so much dedicated to preventing violent jihad but providing channels whereby what is now the *modernity* of jihad can apply its modernity to social interactions – raising the need to give detail and flesh to Ramadan's general recommendation.

The more seamless this modernity, the less there will be an attraction to a 'golden age', a nostalgia, where a pure Muhammad supervised a pure Islamic world. This is what Wahhab sought. He sought it in its purest and starkest form. His descendants found an easy target in the corruption modernity had brought to the House of Saud. In a way, the problem is Saudi Arabia, but in its paradox – whereby it is simultaneously decadent and supports, not so secretly, those who claim piety. Those who are pious have themselves, therefore, made a pact with the devil. They, however, would say they have made a choice whereby the rotting body can nevertheless be used to preserve the embalmed body of the Prophet and his faith. That is perhaps not a choice that the Prophet would, himself, have made.

At this moment in time, without a legitimate caliphate of a 'progressive' Church of England type, or any caliphate at all, there is no centre to the Sunni world outside Mecca. There was, until recently, the possibility of a resurgent leadership emanating from Istanbul under the sometimes-controversial but ostensibly tolerant and community-minded teachings of Gulen.[75] But, with the quarrel between President Erdogan and Gulen, and the latter living in North American exile, the exact contours of how faith interacts with state and the state's relations with other states is unclear. What we have, at the present, is a series of uncertainties in the Islamic world – the barely concealed tensions in Saudi Arabia, as outlined above, being only one.

- There is the question of Iran being opposed by a seemingly contradictory alliance of Saudi Arabia and Israel – the first for confessional reasons and the second for reasons of power politics. An even balance of power seems difficult to envisage with overlays and infusions of religious difference and rhetorical confrontations as well as the courting of Western preferences.

- A tension remains in Egypt, despite the suppression of the Muslim Brotherhood by the militarised government of President Sisi. What was evident was how an unsuccessful but fully formed government under the Brotherhood's President Morsi was able to spring out of the shadows in the wake of the Arab Spring. Required to function in a modern way in running a modern state, it would have been interesting to observe a full term of Morsi's efforts and their effects on an already-present pragmatism within the Brotherhood, and whether this would have grown.[76]

- There remains, above all, the overarching question of institutional representation of God. Can He be approached only via the Church and its interpretation of doctrine? In his youth, Khomeini read and admired the Sufi poets, Shari'ati used them to bridge gaps in his logic with the illumination of metaphor and the sense of driving towards something beyond the material and political sphere. The whirling dervishes who are part of the tourist attractions of Turkey practise, in fact, a method of achieving a transcendental relationship with God – one that is personal, and which transcends not only the conscious persona but also the institutions of material life. It brings into focus the question of personal responsibility before God, and not the devolution of responsibility to a *sura* or an *imam*.

- That sense of individuality versus institutional directives establishes a tension felt by all three religions of the Book; and insofar as institutional directives remain largely paramount, the internal question is the quantities and qualities of literalism and poetry in institutional interpretation. That latter quality of poetry answers the question, 'How many angels can dance on the head of a pin?', with the proposition, 'Show me a hundred different pin heads and I will show you hundreds of different types of angels performing hundreds of different dances'. It is not satisfactory to those who seek absolute anchors. It is ecumenical for those who seek a more tolerant world.

- So, finally, the bedrock question is, in the search for anchors, do we finally seek – like the embalmed bodies of Lenin and Mao – an embalmed God? Or do we seek the spirit who freely created humanity from a speck of dust and made the nations plural?

Chapter 4

Quarrels among the Adherents
of the Same Book

It is far from unusual for interpretations and emphases to differ, sometimes violently, among readers of the same book. Entire overlays of cultures, histories and nationalisms compound the differences until projects of reconciliation – even of dialogue – become fraught endeavours. The religious wars of Europe that led to Kant's hopes for perpetual peace, based on constitutional principles rather than religious ones, echoed right through the twentieth century and into the twenty-first in the confessional divides in Northern Ireland. The violence that marked long episodes of this divide became a kind of 'blue on blue' violence in the name of biblical viewpoints and points of departure.

Often seen as a parallel to Catholic versus Protestant schisms, divisions and violence are those between Sunni and Shi'a in the Islamic world – although these latter have their own complexities which render any loose parallel to the Christian world almost entirely unhelpful.

In this chapter, however, I wish to concentrate on the Sunni-on-Sunni violence seen in conditions of underdevelopment in Africa. Boko Haram in Northern Nigeria predates upon those who subscribe to the same background religious culture. The jihadist insurgency in Mali was against those who believed as the jihadists did and who valued their beliefs in the form of written record in books and libraries – which became targets for the jihadists. Al Shabaab in Somalia struggles against likeminded fellow Somalis.

MALI

Timbuktu in what is now Mali was the site of one of the ancient world's great libraries. Something like what we would recognise as a university was there and was attended by up to twenty-five thousand students. It was a recognised centre of major learning from the thirteenth to the sixteenth century. The city held, and major parts of it still maintain, monumental buildings made of desert-baked mud bricks.[1] If there was one centre of African literate learning, largely Islamic, this was it.[2] It was an African equivalent of the great university of Cordoba from the 700s to 900s in Andalusian Islamic Spain, where the thousands of students, including Christians, sought to study in its great library.[3] Even the English royal family sought to send its offspring to study there.[4] Timbuktu, as a parallel, and with its intellectual riches, should have been a cherished part of Islamic antiquity and a riposte to the assumption that Africa had no cities, no centres of written learning and no libraries.

The seeming jihadist insurrection of 2012 took the Malian authorities by surprise. They had made no military strategies, had apparently little intelligence of the timing and scale of the attack and the military dispositions they could muster after the attack began were insufficient and, above all, cumbersome. The jihadists swept down at speed from the north, took Timbuktu, began ransacking it – including destroying as many ancient manuscripts as they could find (many such manuscripts were saved by heroic librarians)[5] – and were poised to sweep towards the capital city of Bamako. The almost-overnight rapid-response deployment of French forces (Operation Serval) drove them back.

At first sight, it seemed an alliance between jihadists and Tuareg dissidents – also of the same Islamic persuasion, but disillusioned and dissatisfied with the government's lack of effective recognition for their traditional nomadic way of life and claims for greater autonomy in their northern strongholds. The image of pastoralists concerned for their grazing rights allied in the effort to destroy priceless manuscripts built an image of ignorant militants without appreciation for historical culture or settled centres of learning. However, recent scholarship suggests a web of hidden forces, conspiratorial coalitions with political agendas way beyond just a pastoralism and a 'fundamental' Islamicist view of the world.[6] They show violence as both cyclical, not in exact temporal terms but in terms of repeated historical failures adequately to address grievances, and the mobilisation of such forces as are available, including ethnic and religious ones.[7]

Even so, the image of a certain ignorance persisted. Tuaregs do not live in great cities. Many of the fighters would have been illiterate and so their Qur'an was one of recitation rather than interrogation of the written text. Insofar as some currency related to this view may pertain to rank-and-file fighters, it evokes, by way of analogy, a certain Wahhabism – a spartan wish to return to a less complex universe that is simultaneously more equal and, in some ways, 'pure'. In short, such an evocation is a segue into a discussion of underdevelopment and the psychoses on top of material deprivations that occur.

How much of this can be argued and sustained is a question not able to be fully explored in this book. And it is to an extent belied by the reports, not fully confirmed, of overtures on the part of the government to the residual rebels for negotiation – that is, there are agendas for negotiation, even if they appear esoteric or even gnomic to outsiders.[8]

Certainly, the insurrection, even with some purist core, was astounding in its technological modernity – involving fast mobile warfare and Clause-witzian concentration at speed on the weakest points of the enemy. The Browning machine guns mounted on the trays of fast-moving pickups totally out-manoeuvred the slow Malian tanks – which were in any case not well used, being deployed mostly as slowly mobile artillery. All this meant a strategic command among the insurrectionaries which was simply far better generalship than that of the Malian forces. Moreover, the insurrection had an international character, with rear bases in Algeria – a country long riven between militant Islamic and secular forces.

The French intervention was simply based on airlifting, very rapidly, armoured vehicles that could move faster than the pickups of the rebels and were simultaneously more heavily armed.

But, even in a war of technological generalship, in which the rebel gener-als were better than the Malian ones, the sense of a core to the fighting rebel army, one which was well-motivated and with high morale, remains one with at least a possible relationship to what became the caliphate of ISIS (Islamic State of Iraq and Syria) just two years later, in 2014[9] – in which a purist Islamic version of Augustine's City of God was proposed as possible on earth. Timbuktu was then nothing but an impediment, a city of man, an impersonator of what was possible.

Among such rebels, the 'Book' becomes not a book, as such, but a rallying and unifying just cause seeking the intersection between heaven and earth.

By contrast, 'real' debate on the 'Book' can be mundane and rule and ritual ridden, or riven. Thus, here I suggest a possibility of according intelligent and idealistic depth of agency to the illiterate jihadists.

There are, at first sight, less learned circumstances in Nigeria and Soma-lia, in the sense that there is, by way of contrast, no Timbuktu. Except that in Nigeria there were such great cities as Kano and Maiduguri, the latter, in particular, with a resplendent Islamic heritage; and, in Somalia, the Western-inspired overthrow of the Islamic Courts Union was the overthrow of an effort to establish a learned and uniform foundation to the administration, in an anarchic country, of law – of jurisprudence.

SOMALIA

In the first week of August 2022, the Somali government appointed a former al-Shabaab deputy leader and spokesman to the cabinet. Muktar Robow became minister of religious affairs. He had just been released from four years of house arrest for organising a radical militia – an arrest that had sparked riots in which twenty-five people died. Although he had split from al-Shabaab in 2015 this seemed in no way connected with any renunciation of violence. He had expressed the split as one of ideological differences, but it is not clear exactly what these were. He was regarded as sufficiently dangerous, and with sufficient background in committing terror, for the United States to place a price of $5 million on his head (this was withdrawn in 2017).[10]

There were several speculative interpretations of his release and elevation. One suggested an ideological war on al-Shabaab but, as mentioned above, it is unclear exactly what the ideological points of difference might be. They would not be doctrinal in the sense of theological debate but, rather, doctrine as applied to one level or another of struggle, including violent struggle, in the nation's politics. Another view was that release was one thing but bringing him into government was a means of covering up his former crimes committed on behalf of al-Shabaab, and also al-Qaeda, and preventing their recurrence. Or it may simply have been a case of, in the colloquial and colourful words of my ministerial-level informant, bringing him 'inside the tent so he would piss out, rather than his being outside the tent pissing in'. In short, it was a case of reforming someone, or contingently neutralising him, by incorporating him. Or, again in the words of my informant, 'Some kind of deal or trade-off was reached'.

But this, any way it is viewed, means the stuff of political bargaining; yet the Book is not something over which a bargain can be made. This speaks to material, political and negotiable agendas with pragmatism and compromises – perhaps even treacheries. The Book is held in common but is background to the bargains in the foreground.

Could this have been possible in other situations, not only involving other personnel in Somalia but even in places as disparate as Mali or, indeed, Afghanistan? It must be said that, in the case of Somalia, the case of Muktar Robow would have once seemed impossible – not least because of seeming religious 'extremism' but because, also, of the unforeseen legacy of the United Nations (UN) Operation Restore Hope, the wretched incapacities of succeeding interim governments, the prevalence of warlords, the immense and intricate web of clans as the key social organisational device, the Western-sponsored Ethiopian invasion and the overthrow through the Ethiopians of the Islamic Courts Union. Unity of any sort because of any one or several of these factors looked a forlorn hope. But each of these in turn.

Operation Restore Hope made reputations. Bernard Kouchner, who founded Médecins Sans Frontières (Doctors Without Borders) and became a member of the French Cabinet, was filmed conspicuously wading to the Somali shore bearing a sack of relief food across his shoulders. The 'atrocious Somali warlords' who had let their people starve were represented in Hollywood films like *Black Hawk Down* (2001) in which a US military helicopter was shot down by the warlord's forces – showing they had capacity as well as terror and callousness on their side.[11] The black and white representation of starvation, cruelty and Western heroism forever marked all subsequent international approaches to Somalia. Although even the 'Western heroism' was divided, with Italian forces (thinking of knowledge gained in Italy's colonial sojourn in Somalia) not fully cooperating with US forces, despite both being under the UN umbrella.[12] Politics among the peacekeepers/makers mirrored the diverse politics within Somalia itself.

Although most appreciations of the degeneration of Somalia use Operation Restore Hope as a point of departure, Muuse Yuusuf argues that the Ogaden war of 1977 between Somalia and Ethiopia, with the Soviet Union taking the side of Ethiopia, undermined the dictatorship of Siyad Barre to such an extent that any subsequent formal national government became impossible.[13] The loss of the territory meant a fragmentation in the sense of the identity of Somalia – so that the terrifying competitiveness of succeeding warlords spoke not only to the loss of a central dictator but also to a recourse to clan identities that seemed more cohesive than a damaged nationalism. When famine compounded the sufferings of Somalia, and the divided warlords could not agree on a common solution, the UN sought to intervene. In fact, the 1993 *Black Hawk Down* incident occurred in the second phase of the UN's efforts, with an intermediate UN-sanctioned US effort, and lasted from 1993 to 1995.

To the outside world, the famine spoke enough, and the UN was seen as seeking only to redress widespread suffering. In fact, although the military operations sought to engineer the stability that national humanitarian efforts required, they never in actual fact, especially the intervening US effort, moved much beyond security and stability objectives – showpiece photo opportunities like Kouchner's notwithstanding.[14]

The second full UN phase, United Nations Operation in Somalia II (UNOSOM II), four months into its mandate became fully militarised, focused against the armies of the warlord, Mohammed Farah Aidid. At the height of external intervention, thirty-seven thousand troops were deployed, twenty-five thousand of whom were US personnel. But the 1993 incident of the shooting down of the US helicopter showed Aidid's strength[15] – even the 2001 Hollywood film did not really seek to disguise this, and the stuffing was knocked out of the intervention which sought only to hold ground until withdrawal two years later. Extended fracture and, some would say, anarchy followed – although they were cloaked by an interim administration that depicted itself as governmental until 2006 when it was expelled from the capital, Mogadishu, by a consortium that had been slowly but surely gaining national adherence, the Islamic Courts Union (ICU). The US-sponsored Ethiopian invasion that followed in the same year, with its Warsaw Pact tactics of mass destruction as a prelude to military advance, levelled huge parts of Mogadishu and only reinforced the image of Ethiopia as an age-long enemy of Somalia. It destroyed the Islamic Courts Union but, in doing so, released its radical wing from moderating influences and, in the ascendancy of al-Shabaab, the worst fears of the West were realised in what was in a real sense its own creation.[16]

But what the Islamic Courts Union did was to effectively end, or at least curtail, rule by arbitrariness – the right against arbitrariness being a central objective of every constitution on earth – by the uniform application of Islamic law. The ICU also, and this work has also been the accomplishment of al-Shabaab, used faith to act as a unifying carapace over the divisiveness of clans.

Clans, from being not factored into US think-tank analyses at all, to becoming a generalised *bete noir* of the Somali condition, are an extremely complex social-organisational device – and the relationship between different clans is the most complex part of it all. When the government of Kenya sought to mediate in the seemingly never-ending conflicts of Somalia, it managed to assemble almost all the clans together. With Kenyan diplomacy professor, my former student, Makumi Mwagiru as an adviser, the clans were, for the first time, mapped and their relationships and alliances and order of rank were laid out. That mediation was not successful, but it showed what could be possible if all the actors with discernible interests could be recognised. For what al-Shabaab binds together can be pulled apart by these same forces. And the processes of unity or disunity are to do, finally, not with religion (unless perhaps foregrounded with force) but with political bargaining.

Certainly, the extraordinary political forces that bind the disparate parts of al-Shabaab together, and bind it not just by violence to the nation, were described in their complexity and indeed nuance by peacekeeper-cum-scholar Stig Jarle Hansen, who spent time interacting with al-Shabaab leaders and found a profound if not necessarily attractive phenomenon.[17]

So much so that even al-Shabaab might be susceptible to a negotiated inclusion in formally recognised Somali politics. Whether their presence would be problematic, as with Hezbollah in the Lebanese government – whether one can be a sectional militia and a political party in a coalition government simultaneously – or whether the imperatives of at least some progress in nation-building or nation-impersonation might drive a way forward, remains to be seen. But even the Crisis Group speculates on what political engagement might look like.[18] Although, any diplomatically supported engagement would first have to circumvent or address very real international concerns about al-Shabaab's links with al-Qaeda and other groups of international terror. Musee Yusuf notes how such international concerns almost created al-Shabaab as a target, and then the target had to create itself in a certain way.[19] This was certainly a creation outside formal politics, but the Somali situation cannot remain forever bifurcated, so the questions are whether al-Shabaab can adapt to formal politics, whether what is meant to be secular government can accept at least a degree of sharia law, if that is the al-Shabaab conditionality, and whether the international community can accept even a measured adaptation of the disparate parties to each other – whether the international community can, for its own adaptability to any such situation, 'uncreate' its sense of al-Shabaab. These are essentially political questions.

NIGERIA

Nigeria was always an unlikely creation, an amalgamation of large regions that could easily have become nation-states in their own right but which were colonially administered as a unified putative state, and it came to independence as such – entering a sectional civil war shortly after in the late 1960s. The determined and well-conducted national rebuilding and efforts at coherence that came afterwards were regarded as a model[20] – even if the merits of secession are still debated in what was briefly called Biafra and which briefly attracted much international sympathy and some limited support.[21] The sense of bias within the current federal government and the impact of corruption have helped fuel an activist nostalgia for the days of attempted statehood.[22] Certainly, that brief effort at Biafran statehood sought to emulate international practice, both to court international support and also as a binding national force. The Biafran army marched to an anthem drawn from Sibelius's *Finlandia*. The cultivation of Western support also drew from the careful presentation of Biafran secession leader, Chukwuemeka Odumegwu Ojukwu, with his Oxford education, accent and British military training.

If Biafra is still debated, it is debated in terms of Western statehood and capacity for state practice. This is almost entirely absent in the case of the more recent Boko Haram insurrection in the north of Nigeria. It would be hard to imagine one side to a conflict being depicted in the West in more reductionist terms. Even the group's name, Boko Haram, is given the easy and confrontational translation of 'Western learning is forbidden' – although it more literally means 'Falsehood is forbidden'. While this latter meaning certainly challenges Western influences, it also, especially at the dawn of the organisation in 2002, challenges the perceived hegemony of the south in federal politics and the national economy. In this sense of perceived bias, the mantra of an overall Nigerian nationalism was seen as a falsehood. In addition, and more complexly, the efforts of several northern municipalities and regions to use sharia law from 2000 was seen as a corrupted effort – and in this sense, what was forbidden, *boko*, was Islamic falsehood. The Boko Haram armed insurgency didn't begin till 2009 and became internationally infamous with the 2014 kidnapping of the 276 Chibok schoolgirls. But whether in its earlier or later violent phases, two things should be noted: the group reflected a Nigerian north–south divide in political, economic and cultural terms – a comprehensive divide – and the violence of the group, seen by the West as derived from Islamic fundamentalism, was directed against other Islamic believers. It was of course also directed against people who could claim to have been as economically marginalised by the south as the fighters themselves claimed to be. The politics of it all, involving northern politicians seeking formal political influence by informal alliances with radical groups,[23] mean that reductionist readings of the insurrection are unsatisfactory. Even here, however, there should be caution in drawing a political map of the situation in linear terms.[24] Intersections, manoeuvres and betrayals all form a moving target in terms of any finite definitions. If it must be put as simply as possible, then this was done so elegantly in the 2017 public lecture by, and my discussion with, the Emir of Kano, the traditional ruler of an historically important Islamic city and region. For him, holding the lines of both developmental progress and cultural stability meant a dual tightrope act, a complex balancing act.[25] As he said to me privately, 'If I go too far one way, or not far enough another way, people will desert me for the appeal of Boko Haram'. That appeal is anchored in a skilful rendition of grievance based on history and memory – meaning a starting point in the glories of Islamic civilisation, empire, literacy and learning from the eleventh century in a large swathe of what is now Nigeria and Chad.[26] The complicating thing here is that, as with the historically important city of Timbuktu in Mali, the site of Islamic learning that was famed far beyond its borders, historic Islamic cities like Maiduguri are attacked by Boko Haram, and the Emir of Kano was working to ensure his own historic Islamic city was not attacked. But, if the balances between grievance and memory are as fluid as political alliances, then such work must be a constantly vigilant one.

The Nigerian military has not been successful in defeating Boko Haram. This has been due to a combination of ineptitude, corruption and unwillingness – in that several senior officers may well have been complicit in the informal linkages surrounding Boko Haram.[27] In addition, the Nigerian army has scarcely been a good advertisement for itself, accused of raping as many women as Boko Haram itself.[28]

WHAT IS THE EMBODIMENT OF GOD?

It is, of course, both easy and exceedingly generalised to say, 'But that is just Africa'. But all the religions of the Book originated and grew in what were once, and in many cases remain, communities of underdevelopment. The condition of the twentieth century, however, was one where peoples sought independent statehood as a means of self-determining organisation that contrasted with the sense of being over-lorded in the colonial state. What we now call the developmental state means exactly the state as a project in mid-creation. To that sense of emergence, anchors from the past are attached – 'It was glorious once' – which also act as towropes to the future. The anchor and the towrope are renditions of learning that desport themselves as authoritative, time-honoured and within present time as a continuum to the future. The emergent and developmental state is meant to carry history into the future. The test is whether it can be seen to do so authoritatively. Ownership of authority becomes rightful ownership of the state. The developmental state is contested for the sake of its becoming the embodiment of godly purpose.

None of this abolishes a myriad of local agendas, as in all three of the case studies touched on in this chapter. But the state is, finally, viewed by way of, in parallel Christian terms, the 'City of Man' aspiring to be as close as possible to the City of God – giving imperfect body to the perfect City of God.

Chapter 5

Quarrels Involving Those with No Book

The cases of religions without a centralising Book, for example, Buddhism, with antagonisms towards others with or without a Book – as in the cases of Sri Lanka and Myanmar – are discussed in this chapter. A Book is not essential to a national project, but organisational density that reinforces belief – so that belief reinforces the national project – is.

This chapter also examines how a secular state, China, has launched antagonistic policies towards the Islamic Uighur people – and how this may be seen as one aspect of China's incapacity to understand and tolerate movements based on faith. The Uighurs, it may be argued, represent a competing nationalism, but the Falun Gong another much more recent spiritually based movent, cannot be seen in that light. The ingredients of faith within the Falun Gong bypass the state entirely. The state responds as if challenged, as if its organisational density is regarded by the Falun Gong as of no account.

In received wisdom, especially in the developed West, Buddhism is seen as a religion of serenity and tranquillity. It is seen as an antidote to the violent psychological stresses of industrialised and commodified competitive life. In the vogue of replicating (and sometimes straight-up looting) Tibetan figurines and statues of Buddhist saints and *bodhisattva* (those who renounce Nirvana to be endlessly reborn to ease human suffering) in the early 2000s, there was a forgetfulness or elision of the Tibetan recognition that the serene creatures of the spiritual universe could have a reverse décor. They could become fiery and almost monstrous in their anger.[1] And, indeed, the early history of Buddhism – certainly as expressed in the legends that grew out of this history – is cleanly separated from its modern purpose of serenity; but Ashoka, who united almost all the Indian subcontinent between 300 and 200 BC, was also a great advocate and proselytiser of Buddhism, despite the immense bloodiness of the wars of unification and the reputation of the exquisitely refined pain he administered to his defeated enemies in his torture chambers.

The motif of Buddhism as nationalistic and bloody infuses modern history as well. A 'fundamentalist Buddhism' may have as much for which to answer as 'fundamentalist Islam', notwithstanding the laziness of such terms to describe complex animations and rationales. But bloodiness and callousness – the latter as opposed to an almost stereotypical 'compassion' – are markers of two recent dramas of modern history in which Buddhism was a major force.

To begin with an anecdote: in 1979 I was in Colombo helping to host an international conference that featured many of the then–'golden generation' of young Sri Lankan ministers, as well as visiting governmental delegations, many on their way to Manila, where critical global trade talks were to be held. We designed the Colombo event in part as a briefing point for these delegations. But, of the local hosts, the dashing minister of youth, Ranil Wickremesigne, was the one destined to become prime minister and attempt to end the terrible conflict that had broken out between the government with its dominant Sinhalese population, and the Tamil Tigers. He at least achieved a pause in the conflict, and it always seemed to me he had risen from an inconspicuous portfolio because many of his colleagues were exploded by Tamil Tiger bombs. In 1979, with the first signs of war clouds looming, he arranged for me to be included in a small group to meet the prime minister, Ranasinghe Premadasa, who served under President Junius Jayewardene. The president had crafted an international image of himself as a serene Buddhist leader of placid wisdom. I rose to speak and said that the global community was gravely concerned about the prospect of war in a country admired for its love of peace and that surely it was not too late for negotiations with the Tamil community.

Premadasa's response was a superbly expressed and modulated expression of Buddhist condescension – which I have never forgotten – with the lines, 'young man, you should not concern yourself with things that you cannot understand'. My career in the years afterwards included understanding at least war and its devastation only too well. And, although I never involved myself either in assessing the war in Sri Lanka or the fruitless efforts to broker a lasting peace, I was only too aware of what lay behind the casualty figures compiled by others. And I came to also understand at least some of the motivations and senses of agency of female Tamil fighters and suicide bombers,[2] as I met and later helped 'reintegrate' female (and male) fighters into 'society' after other conflicts. As it was, a female Tamil suicide bomber did for Indian Prime Minister Rajiv Ghandi (and herself), when he could have been a key to a more moderate approach in regional relations, especially with the warming *détente* with Pakistan, then led by an equally young and hopeful

Benazir Bhutto. Somehow, I never forgave the Tamil Tigers for that assassination, but they would argue, with great conviction and convincingly, that they were seriously wronged by the Sinhalese and Buddhist government in Colombo, and any seeming friend of Colombo was no friend of theirs.

For a dominant group to build a nationalism, there must be a series of binding forces. Having the largest population of the different groups is not enough, unless there is both a group purpose and a group rationale – and that rationale must be based on an ethical explanation for their continued if not perpetual dominance. And that ethical explanation must have an institutional expression that is part of everyday life – so that dominance is simply 'normal' as well as justified by the everyday institutional expression of ethical rationale.

In Sri Lanka, there is the added factor of colonial history when it was the Sinhalese kingdom centred in Kandy that brokered arrangements, first with the Dutch to help defeat the Portuguese and then with the British who succeeded the Dutch after capturing Kandy. In the case of the British it took until the twentieth century, however, under Governor Sir William Manning in the 1920s, explicitly to favour the Sinhalese elites over those of the Tamil population in terms of modern constitutional arrangements that prefigured self-government. So independence, when it came in 1948, came with a Sinhalese constitutional domination as well as a 73 per cent domination of the population. It took protracted negotiations within the newly independent state for the Tamils to secure some measure at least of constitutional rights.

But what also bound the Sinhalese project – Ceylon, then Sri Lanka, as inherently Sinhalese – together was the matter of religion and the coordination of the monastic institutions. The priestly class and the political class became allies. Who more used whom is a debate, but in any case the ethical rationale for domination lay in subscription to Buddhism as an organised religion of supreme ethical content, bespeaking an organised civilisation that was peculiar to the island of Sri Lanka – whereas the Tamils, a minority in any case, were regarded as historical interlopers from southern India, only 54.8 kilometres (34 miles) separating the northern tip of Sri Lanka and the southern coast of India, and the Hindu religion was more disparate in its organisation and the characteristics of its different gods. Although it should be pointed out that the Tamil community has a sense of differentiation between a core of people, long enough in place to claim themselves as the originator of the nation, and more recent Tamil migrants from India, many were imported by the colonial authorities as workers on the plantations.

Kandy, the epicentre of Sinhalese historical identity, was far closer to Colombo, the independence capital, than Jaffna, the historical city of the Tamils on the north coast – so that, quite apart from political domination at high level, it was easier to fill junior civil service positions from the local population of Colombo, and this local population was largely Sinhalese. And the 'move' from Kandy to Colombo seemed an easy transition of only 117 kilometre (73 miles). The idea of Colombo as a Sinhalese capital (of a Sinhalese state) was reinforced by a succession of independence prime ministers and presidents who were Sinhalese – and, even though some of these had a genuinely inclusive sense of citizenship, their origin was in itself symbolic of power as located within the Sinhalese. Sinhala became the official national language.

The debates on class, poverty and deprivation – for Sri Lanka was far from egalitarian in terms of its economy and distribution of wealth – could be ameliorated by senses of unity in religion – especially as a pan-Tamil/Sinhalese working-class movement never achieved headway. The universities of Sri Lanka never played a major role in Sri Lankan politics or in forming public opinion, and members at least of the independence elite had no choice but to obtain their degrees or law qualifications in Britain. The only university (University of Ceylon) was founded as late as 1942 and was not joined by other universities until 1972. Later prime ministers like Ranil Wickremesinghe, born nearly at the time of independence, did obtain their university qualifications from within Sri Lanka. But the sense of a fully nationally engendered intelligentsia was not part of the Sri Lankan experience in its formative national project.

But, within the new state, there was no guarantee that Buddhism as the Sinhalese religion would be a placid and acquiescent partner of the government. Monks could be difficult, to the extent that the fourth prime minister of the independent country, the Oxford-trained Solomon West Ridgeway Dias Banadaranaike, was assassinated in 1959 by a Buddhist monk disgruntled with government funding for his school. Fatally wounded, he asked in 'true' Buddhist fashion on his deathbed for the monk to be forgiven. The monk, after a lengthy judicial process, was hanged anyway; and Banadaranaike was succeeded by his wife, Sirima Ratwatte Dias Banadaranaike, who became the world's first female prime minister, serving three terms and seeking to institute a comprehensive socialist and nationalisation programme – which favoured the Sinhalese, leading to grave tensions with the Tamil population. Because she was regarded in the West as a new phenomenon, a female leader, and a Buddhist one to boot, few outside Sri Lanka noticed the storm clouds looming between the Sinhalese and the Tamils. The tremors of civil war began under the tenure in office of her successors. Her second term ended in 1977, and she was succeeded as prime minister by Jayewardene, who was in turn succeeded by Premadasa. But these successors went to great pains to consolidate and develop work that had begun under her administrations, and that was to secure the support of the monasteries and the monks, effectively seeking the monasteries as validators and endorsers of the Sinhalese state and utilising this as decisive value-added in winning Sinhalese support for the escalating and terrible violence to come. Banadaranaike herself, in her third term, 1994 to 2000, presided over the by-now ongoing standoff with the Tamils.

Roshan de Silva Wijeyeratne has described in detail this process of ensuring monastic support and how Prime Minister Premadasa and President Jayewardene were deeply involved.[3] The two were at the helm of power for many years, Jayewardene being prime minister from 1977/1978 before his presidency of 1978 to 1980, being succeeded by Premadasa as prime minister in 1978. So that when Premadasa chided me for being unable to understand the Sri Lankan situation he was correct in that the institutional mobilisation for war – a mobilisation of church and state – was in its detail and long preparation impenetrable to a visitor. The war, when it broke out in all its fury, went on from 1983 to 2009, with a brief pause from 2001 to 2004.

Wijeyeratne describes a precolonial Buddhism as inclusive in a cosmic sense – that is, it reached out with universal values in which all were included. The era of colonialism, but also of the nationalism that developed as a reaction to it – the desire for independence – became precisely a process of exclusion. The 'superiority' of Buddhist knowledge became conflated with the superiority of the Sinhalese as an ethnic group – so that the 'epistemology' of nationalism became the epistemology of a modern Buddhism. Power and knowledge began to move together, but both were concentrated inwards. Precolonial values were reevaluated and, in Wijeyeratne's words, a new political 'imaginary', allied also to an imaginary of achieving modernity, achieved epistemological hegemony. It became 'impossible' to think in another way except that the projects of independence, government and modern development were projects of the Buddhist Sinhalese. In this capture of Buddhist cosmology, the Tamil became the 'other', an antithesis of both knowledge and progress, and an impediment to ownership of the state. The Tamil could be frowned upon politically and looked down upon as unknowledgeable.[4]

Thus, when the Tamils began to mobilise to achieve, by force of arms, if necessary, a political space in which they could have equivalence to the Sinhalese, the response of the government was not only to think that rebellion should be crushed but also that rebellion would necessarily, in the natural and logical orders of things, be crushed. The war had its ebbs and flows. The Tamils essentially invented the suicide bomber and targeted senior members of the Sinhalese ruling class. Premadasa was targeted and exploded by a suicide bomber in 1993. By that time, he had served as prime minister from 1978 to 1989, and president from 1989 to his death. But the final scale of the eventual victory by the Sinhalese state, with appalling casualties seemingly inflicted without mercy upon the Tamil forces,[5] echoes in the still highly conditional postwar efforts to achieve a 'reconciliation' and some form of 'inclusivity', but all without any penetrating sense of remorse that a nation was deeply and deliberately wounded. And wounded to a fully discernible extent by Buddhism.

Only in the second prime ministerial term of Wickremesinghe from 2001 to 2004 was there a brief pause in hostilities as he sought some negotiated way forwards – that was finally made impossible by his successors – but it was his brief first term in 1993/1994 that saw the assassination of Premadasa. Wickremesinghe's search for peace was therefore backgrounded by full knowledge of the costs of war.

But the search for peace had to contend with the mutually reinforcing senses of cultural and institutional superiority and achieved hegemony. The Sinhalese nation had become the Sri Lankan state. Religion validated this. There is a direct parallel, albeit with its own complex and peculiar aspects, in the case of Myanmar – as Burma, also part of British India.

There are more than one hundred ethnic groups in Myanmar – the well-known example of the Rohingya should not obscure the fact that many have faced problems of marginalisation and discrimination at the hands of the dominant Bamar (whose name gave rise to the British use of 'Burma', already in colonial times identifying one people as the state itself). The Bamar constitute 68 per cent of the population, but 90 per cent of the population are Buddhist, and the most significant cases of resistance and rebellion involve those who are neither Bamar nor Buddhist. The Rohingya, being Islamic, are a minority, therefore, on two fronts. They are also not constitutionally recognised as an ethnic group, whereas the Karen, with their own long history of conflict with the Bamar domination of the state, are. The Karen are also predominantly Buddhist and do not now seek a separate state but a place within a federal Myanmar structure. But they, in short, have a negotiating position within a framework of constitutional recognition for their existence. Theoretically, the Rohingya do not exist – not, in any case, as a constitutional entity. And this derives from the legal framework of Myanmar that accords full recognition only to those settled ethnic groups that inhabited the country before the British annexation of it into colonial India in 1823.

This annexation had its own lieutenant governor, but Burma separated from India in 1937 – amidst clear Japanese moves towards expansionism throughout South and Southeast Asia; and Burma was to become a particularly vicious theatre of war, dragging in not only British but also Indian, Nationalist Chinese and even Zambian troops against the Japanese. The Japanese had their own local support, as they did also in India – promising an end to British colonialism; and Aung San sided with the Japanese as a result. He did later play a key role in negotiating independence from the British but was assassinated in 1947. His legacy, in terms of a powerful family's role in politics, was in the form of his daughter, Aung San Suu Kyi. With war's end, India moved rapidly to independence in 1947, and Burma in 1948 – Burma with two giant surviving figures, U Nu and Ne Win. U Nu led the country at independence, Ne Win, a general, became his successor but later seized power unconstitutionally as the two men and their families waged a struggle for domination of the state. If Ne Win represented the military tendency to enter politics, U Nu became a Buddhist monk while remaining active in politics until his death in 1995. By then, in 1989, Burma had changed its name to Myanmar. The early history of the independent state of an oscillation between two strong rival personalities, and the role of powerful families, was followed by strong militarised and religious factions vying for power in the later state. And, given the meaning of the word 'Myanmar', derived directly from the word 'strong', meaning essentially the strong Bamar, neither church nor army, nor powerful families, despite their contestation, in any way doubted the ethnic and religious hegemony of Bamar and Buddhism within the state.

Military occupation of the government has been a rotating fixture of Myanmar political history. But when, in 2007, the military government made unpopular economic decisions, including the lifting of subsidies, it was the Buddhist monks who led the protests in a tremendous nationwide mobilisation that left the military stunned. And although the protests were eventually suppressed, they played a huge role in public pressure for a return to democracy and the release of Aung San Suu Kyi, in 2010, after many years under house arrest for her own efforts to resist military government. She became a prime ministerial figure in the civilian government that nonetheless always had the military in the background. Even so, the role of the monks was pivotal because of their national organisational base. The British ambassador to Myanmar in 2007, Mark Canning, told me that the common cause of democracy, civilian rule and religious idealism expressed from this organised institutional foundation – that is, the monasteries – made for an incredibly congested alliance, but it was key to eventual change.[6]

The military, remaining in the background, effectively co-opted Suu Kyi, pressing her into an apologist's service as the army set about the forceful suppression of what was described as armed rebellion amongst the Rohingya – long weary with their isolated status and being denied constitutional rights. Suu Kyi, who had become a feminist icon and a perceived champion of democracy, seemed to have become a Buddhist chauvinist with no tolerance of an Islamic minority and the huge refugee problem – particularly for neighbouring Islamic Bangladesh – caused by military actions against them.

She seemed to reveal biases on her visit to Hungary in 2019. Perhaps it was a clumsily judged effort to appeal to Prime Minister Viktor Orbán's own prejudices, but she said that 'the greatest challenge at present for both countries [Myanmar and Hungary] and their respective regions – Southeast Asia and Europe – is migration linked to the continuously growing Muslim populations'.[7]

The military seized power once again at the beginning of 2021, and again imprisoned Aung San Suu Kyi, but this time the monks were divided. Younger monks protested again against the seizure of democracy, but the military had, in advance, got to great lengths to win over the senior clerics, advancing a united front of senior military and senior Buddhists.[8] Both were also solidly united in the effort to reduce Rohingya protest to trouble-free proportions and were not unhappy that so many Rohingya had fled to Bangladesh. Firebrand characters with a popular base, such as the radical anti-Muslim monk Wirathu, were released from prison (where he had been charged with sedition against the civilian government) and made a common cause for the military.[9] He had earlier even urged a 'Buddhist fundamentalism' in Sri Lanka, as the Sinhalese fought against the Tamils.

The form of Theravada-inclined Buddhism in Myanmar – that is, Buddhism of the temple-based and rule-based variety (as in Tibet) – meant a church counterpart to military organisation. One can stand against the other, but the two together become a monolithic expression of state and Buddhist nationalism. Aung San Suu Kyi was herself a captive of this very nationalism, and her sense of nationalist patriotism would have meant she was unable, much to the consternation of her erstwhile international admirers, to defend the Rohingya – least of all from her own military and its church support. And, because the Rohingya were a chronically underdeveloped community, the lack of educational provision and therefore advancement was conflated in the dominant imagination with an inherent backwardness caused by the backwardness of Islam as a religion – a conservative and retarding religion evidenced in a circular fashion by the retarded state of development in the lands of the Rohingya. They were, simultaneously, not ethnically part of Myanmar, uneducated, backwards and followers of a backwards religion. Discrimination formed a composite entity, all aspects of which were portrayed in a negative light and each predetermined in the Bamar imagination of 'self and other' to reinforce one another.

The need for condescension, sustainable only from a platform of 'manifest' superiority, is noteworthy in the cases of Sri Lanka and Myanmar, as the platform stands on spiritual foundations. This may certainly involve a misuse of Buddhism in the cooperative and inclusive form propounded by, for example, the Dalai Lama – but China is deeply wary of Buddhism in precisely its inclusive form as a political force in Tibet – that is, it is inclusive enough to attract international support. In short, one does not have to hate, one might be committed to love, but the political uses of organised Buddhism may be seen in more than one sense.

Tibetan Buddhism, precisely because of the personality and calm charisma of the Dalai Lama, has generated a wave of international interest in the multiple personalities of the Tibetan spiritual universe. Integrated into the indigenous *bon* beliefs of Tibet as Buddhism migrated northwards from India, it became a Buddhism with a pantheon of godly figures: *bodhisattvas* or constantly reincarnated saints who renounce Nirvana for the intrinsically futile mission of easing human suffering, *tara* or female spiritual figures, and even *yidam* whereby through meditation and worship one may create one's own godhead. It was a religion open to preferences, all the same subordinated to an ethos of serenity and compassion. But that meant it was also a moving target. There was no central 'god' that could be traduced. And the plenitude of uncentralised 'gods' migrated into China itself: the *bodhisattva* Avalokitsvara became the Chinese goddess Guan Yin, the personification of mercy.[10] An attack on the characters of the Tibetan spiritual universe is an attack on oneself – a concept not fully eradicated in the secular onslaught of Communism. And even though, or precisely because, the Dalai Lama gives cover to a Tibetan exile leadership with its own political 'hardliners', for whom independence from China is non-negotiable, the Chinese government deems it suitable to focus its attack on this singular readily identifiable character. Because the Dalai Lama is also the head of an organised branch of Buddhism, Theravada, a priestly and temple-led Buddhism, the Chinese include in their campaign the marginalisation of the Tibetan temples and the reduction of their autonomous action.

But the temples can forge no military alliances. What passed for a Tibetan army was vanquished with ease as the Chinese marched into Tibet in 1950, occupying it partially, and then fully with the Dalai Lama fleeing to India in 1959.[11] The Tibetans had resisted modernisation, including of its army, until two years before the Chinese incursion. Chinese propaganda spoke of a feudal and backwards society, needing liberation from both social and antiquarian backwardness. The analysis of society was acute, the method to end its backwardness was high-handed. But what the situation demonstrated was that institutional resistance, and institutional service to the practice of state nationalism, had to be not only well organised but also modern. The Chinese army, organised, drilled and blooded, often bloodied, in the war against Japan and in the Communist conquest of China, had learned the hard way – as had the Nationalist Chinese armies – that lack of modernity against a highly industrialised enemy was a recipe for disaster.

Having said that, what the Dalai Lama has subsequently accomplished is to speak for a nation with ethical and spiritual qualities – in his accounts historically validated for independence as a state – and propose, by spiritual charisma, the union of church and independent state. The Chinese to an appreciable extent do not know what to do. The Lama gives them nothing

solid to oppose and overcome; even the Tibetan Buddhist 'gods' are disparate and diversified; and in attacking the Lama the Chinese are seen to be
attacking the ethical qualities he disseminates to a worldwide audience. It is
a masterclass of nationalism without a state or even a prospect of one.

The Chinese rest their case, finally, not just on overcoming backwardness
or the contestation of spirituality but on historical ownership from imperial
to Nationalist Republican epochs, the Communist epoch merely succeeding
those that preceded it in their claims that Tibet is part of China. The Tibetan
nationalists contest that claim, but the same Chinese claim of historical pos-
session also applies, of course, to Xinjiang heartland of the Uighur population. As in Tibet, there is an historical non-Han Chinese majority population,
so that ethnic and linguistic nationalism can act as counterweight to any
imposed state-decreed nationalism. But in Xinjiang there is also the matter of
religion that has a vast organised international hinterland, and that is Islam.
Affiliated in part to the neighbouring Turkic, Transcaucasian Islamic world,
it has regional links outside of China.

As in Tibet, China seeks to flood the area with Han Chinese settlers who
also seek to dominate the area economically.[12] But, unlike in Tibet, the recent
Chinese programme to crush and control political dissidence by vast 're-
education' schemes in facilities that certainly resemble concentration camps
is also to create a new Uighur personality, shorn of religious prioritisation in
senses of self, loyal to China and to the Communist Party, or at least meekly
acquiescent to them, and without any sense of separate destiny or imagination of separate destiny. What is at stake is not only a remoulding of the
legacies of the past but also a full redirection of the future. The ambition is
matched only by its heavy-handedness. And, in terms of Islam itself, the aim
is to peripheralise it from any national role. What remains problematic is
that Islam has an inescapable international role, and this role has an anchor
– heavily debated, often violently – as a religion of the Book. The Book can
still be an authoritative nodal point of rebellion – but, thus far, the Chinese
have not sought to ban the Book. Even in the most vulgar Communist strategies, that would seem to be biting off more than even the mighty Chinese
state can chew.

The Book has a hinterland of interstate support. In international relations
this can be more important than mere international support of the kind the
Dalai Lama commands. The Chinese are careful not to create any sustainable impression of a genocide against the Uighurs – although this has been
an accusation used against the Chinese – in recognition that an umma, an
international community with state as well as religious foundations, might
turn against China. The Falun Gong, on the other hand, has no such hinterland, although it is certainly trying through cultural means to create the
basis of international support. Its principal vehicle is its traditional dance and

musical performance troupe. This tours the world, and its major iteration is called Shen Yun. These troupes are not advertised as part of the Falun Gong, although no effort is made to hide the link. The self-advertised meaning of the name, Shen Yun, is 'divine beings dancing'. This is poetic. My sense of a literal translation is simply 'divine person' or 'cosmic person'. But the dancing and other aspects of the lengthy stage show are superb. 'Divine dancing' would not escape the superlatives heaped by many theatre critics on what they do. In my opinion, the performances are better than those staged by official Chinese state-supported troupes, and, that is to say, they exceed a high bar. The advertising for the shows, tour by tour, has become more blatant in its messaging. Shen Yun is advertised as 'China before Communism'. The more the People's Republic persecutes the group, the more oppositional it becomes. It was more subtle in its self-statements even half a decade ago.[13] Then, the only clue that it was Falun Gong–related was, usually only in one song, lyrics related to 'Buddhist *fa*', translated on screen as 'Buddhist law'. In fact, there is no such thing insofar as it evokes, for example, a Mosaic 'law' such as one of the Ten Commandments. It is more an esoteric, almost gnomic reference to a Buddhist cosmic nature in which Enlightenment sits. But, either as law or nature, the *fa* supersedes any other law. And that is precisely the Falun Gong's problem with the People's Republic of China – its prioritisation of *fa*.

The Falun Gong, which originated in the 1990s, has a membership largely of Han Chinese. Its mystic centrepieces are entirely Chinese. Apart from Buddhism, there is a fair admixture of Taoism, and the central membership practice of Qi Gong, a series of exercises related to Tai Chi, is directly concerned with channelling the energy of the cosmos through one's body, linking the body to the cosmos.[14] That linkage is transcendental – that is, there is no need for the practitioner to have an intervening institution such as a political party or a state. It is the bypassing of both party and state – and it was the bypass, not opposition in the first instance – that raised the eyebrows and then the hackles of the Chinese authorities. If anything, quite unlike the Islam of the Uighurs or the Buddhism of the Tibetans, the Falun Gong is *too* Chinese, making the People's Republic look like a modern interloper. It implicitly questions the chanted prayer of Mao as he received the march of the victorious People's Liberation Army in Tienanmen Square in 1949. At that moment of victory, using antique language in the style of the old shamans, Mao claimed the 'Mandate of Heaven'. For the Falun Gong, everyone has the mandate of heaven.

Having said all that, the movement is now headquartered in the United States, where its founder, Li Hongzhi, also now lives.[15] In its American guise, it has become increasingly right wing in terms of its media presence –primarily through its newspaper, the *Epoch Times* – and biased towards conspiracy theories and anti-evolution creationism. Whether this is to garner a particular type of already anti-Communist American support is an open question. But it is its position in China itself that speaks to the Chinese government's inability to deal with religion as any type of organisation autonomous of the party and the state. Religions of the Book that have an associated nationalism – that is, a nationalism that rivals or might rival that propagated by Beijing – seem a special threat, but something more amorphous like the mysticism of the Falun Gong is also seen as a threat. In short, anything with provision for a rival affiliation, a rival dense loyalty to that owed the Chinese Communist Party and the state, is a threat.[16]

But outside of China, the declared peacefulness of Buddhism has a tarnished record when attached to its own state projects that are also ethnically and religiously exclusive. Within and without China, it is Islam that has suffered. The religion of the Book is excoriated in Myanmar as much as it is in Xinjiang by the Chinese.

Chapter 6

The Impossibility of Life Outside the Realm of the Book

In his intellectual biography of Edward Said, Timothy Brennan summarised Said's observation that Zionism 'had always presented itself as an "unchanging idea" and had now acquired doctrinal solidity in the form of a state'.[1] The key element here is that the state is doctrinally formed, even though originally proposed as secular, and what I seek to discuss in this chapter is the essence of doctrine in a religio-historical animation and justification that resists change even while persisting with the advertisement of itself as secular. We are examining here the weight of an infallible history, made more so by trauma, and the sense that the founding of the state of Israel was a form of redemption and a return to a history that was interrupted. The material purpose of the state is to resume its mythical borders, as described in the Judaic 'Book', to complete both history/destiny and to do so without apology or regret. In this sense, the Arab/Palestinian resistance confronts a stolid and solid monolith. The state itself becomes the embodied God.

The equivalence of state with 'God's state' is apparent also in the rise and convictions of the American Christian right – although here we see God's purpose as compellingly Protestant, as enunciated by Max Weber in an earlier part of this book. Here we see human agency, because righteous – because abstemious and diligent, industrious – establish a benchmark for how one achieves both the blessing of the state and the blessing of God. The state may not bless or reward those who are not industrious, and the state, while far short of the 'City of God', is nevertheless a prototype of the City of God. Even the melodic metaphor, 'from sea to shining sea', echoes Augustine's images of majestic light in the City of God. In this sense of not only faith, but fidelity to how God wishes a state to be, the United States becomes the sacred leader of all other states in the world. It too becomes, if not the embodied

God, the embodiment of the purpose of God and, as such, marries itself to its
sister state in God, the state of Israel.

There is a scene in King Vidor's hugely popular but over-wrought 1959 epic
film, *Solomon and Sheba* – with Yul Brynner and his Transcaucasian looks
as Solomon and Gina Lollobrigida with her smouldering Italian looks as
Sheba – in which Solomon takes a solitary walk in the courtyard of the great
temple he has built and contemplates his work. Although the Old Testament
gives a description of the temple, its appearance in the film seems modelled
on Herod's later temple. Solomon's temple, even while it depended on the
cedars of Lebanon, donated by King Hiram of Tyre as a gesture of good international relations, was the marker that the Kingdom of Israel had 'arrived'.
Israel was a state with a capital city and that capital city housed an epicentre
of purpose and validation: the children of Israel were the children of God
as evidenced by the temple. Israel had achieved consolidation as a state like
its neighbours and rivals. Samson had, after all, torn down the pillars of the
Philistine temple but, until Solomon, Israel had no equivalent. Now it had one
better than any other.

   It also had a king who, as well as building the temple, was internationally
revered for his wisdom – not only in matters of (literally) proportionate justice but in terms of the natural sciences such as zoology and botany. The ideas
of wisdom, justice and laws as markers of a state were again emphasised
when, after the Persians released the Israelites from Babylonian captivity, the
return to the homeland was marked not only by the rebuilding of the temple
destroyed by the Babylonians – although the new structure was originally
more modest than Solomon's – but also by Ezra and his cohort of priests offi-
cialising an account of a long history as a nation, and codifying laws and state
practice. The temple was given a renewed grandeur by Herod (not the Herod
of the time of Jesus) and stood from 516 BC to AD 70 before its destruction
by the Romans after the siege of Jerusalem, and its tearing down was a mark
that the Jewish revolt for an independent state had been brought to its knees.
The population was dispersed to other parts of the Roman Empire, so that
there was not only no longer a state with a central marker but there was also
no longer a nation in place. Jerusalem, as rebuilt by the Ottoman Empire,
features a mosque where the temple once stood.

   As for Solomon's kingdom, we have in fact no supportive documentary
evidence that Solomon existed, but the biblical account of his state expansionism saw this as accomplished not only by warfare but by diplomatic alliances – commemorated by his marrying the daughters of other kings. These
wives were later reputed to have led him 'astray', influencing him with their
own religious practices, so that the expanded kingdom became fragile in
its internal coherence, Solomon giving room to alternative gods rather than

anchoring the state on the 'one true God'. But the legendary Solomonic kingdom, thus achieved, at its greatest extent became the precedent for an *eretz*
Israel, a Greater Israel. Yet even Solomon in all his diplomatic wisdom and
pragmatism could not sustain his extensive borders. And, both in his time
and the times of his successors, the kingdom condensed and then split and
never recovered its legendary grandeur. *Eretz* Israel, even in legend, was a
momentary affair.

But it is precisely the legends of origin – exodus from slavery in Egypt and
the slow maturity to magnificent statehood – that impart parameters of belief:
an ordained land of freedom and, finally, a hegemonic space for a state. The
condition of hegemony was reinforced as a centrally desirable condition by
later events in the history of the Jewish people.

Much, of course, transpired between Solomon and the foundation of modern Israel. Captivity in Babylon was something from which recovery was
possible. Curiously, it seemed no one else had settled in the territory during
the exile in Babylon. The dispersal that followed the Roman subjugation of
the Jewish revolt in AD 70 led, as discussed earlier in this book, to an almost
two-thousand-year era of the 'wandering Jew', the majority settlement of the
territory by others (although some pockets of Jewish habitation survived) and
the eventual development in Europe of a rich Yiddish culture and a vibrant
cultural life, even if often in segregated quarters. It preserved a group cultural
identity among the European Jews.[2] This was not necessarily replicated, and
certainly not in the same way among the 'oriental' or Mizrahi/Sephardi Jews
who developed their own communities in Arabic and North African Islamic
territories. Mizrahi/Sephardi Jews are, strictly speaking, two lineages now
often conflated into a single grouping to differentiate them from European
Jews.[3] Their descendants form about 61 per cent of the Jewish population of
Israel, and their immediate ancestors were expelled from places like Iraq after
the defeat of the Arab armies in the first Arab–Israeli war. They suffered their
own discriminations and persecutions, but the over-riding motif of modern
Jewish suffering, directly related to the felt need for a state of both freedom
and hegemony, was the European Holocaust. This defines all political space
in international debate on the status of Israel and has also given rise to the
appellation of 'anti-Semitic' for those who oppose the current Jewish state,
or even its policies towards non-Jews.

Orthodoxy also originated in Europe, and the bedrock of international
support for Israel is derived from Europe and the United States with its own
European lineages and Jewish population. But, despite many centuries of
European habitation and, in many instances, conspicuous social and economic success by Jewish people in mainstream society, the Holocaust was
not simply a Nazi German project but one with pan-European complicity in
all the Nazi-conquered territories. The image of isolated communities often

belies marked absorption of European culture. In the concentration camps, orchestras formed by the inmates – sometimes literally playing for their lives to entertain their guards – revealed repertoires of the finest European compositions. Yet, although many people risked their lives – sometimes very heroically – to save Jewish fellow citizens, they can be identified almost individually in, for example, memorials to the 'righteous gentiles' or 'righteous among the nations'. It must be said that in no country was there a blanket wall of resistance from the majority of the population on behalf of the Jews. It is that sense of large aloneness, as well as the terrible industrial deaths and torture, that marked the Jewish psyche. World War II and the death camps remain a living memory for people who endured and survived them and whose generation has not yet passed away, and whose state was to a huge extent founded on their scars.

Those scars were huge. Across Europe the Jews were deported to concentration camps and millions died in them – their deaths recorded in a meticulous 'banality of evil', an accounting process as well as an industrial one.[4] It also led to a huge literature, seeking to describe both the heroism of those in the camps and those who managed to escape being rounded up and went into the forests to fight. Even Hollywood, finally, after years of depicting Jews only as victims, starred Daniel Craig in a film about the WWII fighting Jew.[5] It was that sense of fight that Jews took to the postwar Israel that Europe endorsed, at least partly out of guilt. But was it only a legacy of guilt?

Samuel Goldman represents a generation of scholars in the United States who perceive what he calls a 'Christian Zionism', in which a species of American Christianity draws much of its shape from the biblical history and apparent prophecies of the future for the Jews; and that the two are parallel expressions of the same godly will that binds the two nations of the United States and modern Israel – the latter having a direct link to the historical and biblical Israel.[6]

Separately, but within this impulse, it is perhaps no coincidence that a peculiarly American scripture, the Book of Mormon, should essentially replicate the biblical account of Israel in America.

Goldman says that the idea of covenant binds the two nations – that is, God has covenanted with both and both are chosen and blessed by Him; biblical prophecy promises a Jewish return to the Holy Land, which is holy also to Christians as the site of God's will and the return of Jesus; and there are shared social values – not least because many of the leaders of Israel were drawn not only from Europe but from the United States. Repeated prime minister Netanyahu, although born in Tel Aviv, lived many years as a child in the United States, and took degrees from MIT. When he speaks on television, it is with a conspicuous American accent. To American viewers, he is one of them.[7]

There is a clear sense that many Protestant Christians in the United States also have a parallel 'Zionist' vision of themselves: the Pilgrim Fathers having delivered themselves from persecution and finding a Promised Land of their own. The deliverance of the Jews from the Holocaust, aided in part by American soldiers who liberated some of the concentration camps, led to a sense that the Jews were again being released from a house of slavery, a modern, more atrocious Egypt, and that it was a reiteration of the biblical saga of Moses that, once again, they should inherit the land of Israel, with the United States both as its chaperone and modern forebear, its parallel, in achieving deliverance. This much is reasonably stated. It is the building not only of a modern state that triumphed over many difficulties and powerful enemies – the Americans against the British in the war of independence also being a parallel to the Jewish survival in the face of the Nazis – but also the building of a modern hegemonic state that requires comment. A hegemony sanctioned and reinforced with 'God on our side'. The segue from survival to hegemony depends on being a state – which becomes both an organisational and validating device, in turn requiring validation as part of its justification.

Survival needing power is part of an equation. Having enemies requires greater power than they have. The defeat of enemies or accommodation with them does not mean the scaling back of power and reserves of power, but the same means and capacity of power are directed against new enemies or lesser enemies. Or, both large enemies and problematically smaller ones may be engaged at the same time. Achieving a recognised vocation of power requires the ability to face down both. In the case of the United States, there are the two large rivals, if not enemies, in China and Russia. In the case of Israel, Iran is seen as a potential nuclear rival and thus a threat; and the Palestinians may be treated differently but still with a hegemonic ruthlessness whenever required. Emerging from a 'house of bondage' mandates the mission of never going back into it – whether any real or perceived enemy wants you to go back into it.

But to exercise hegemonic power over an enemy requires that enemy to have the capacity and characteristics to 'receive' power. It requires the enemy to have state, or at least quasi-state, institutions that can be affected and harmed by power. This is why the United States in particular had so much difficulty identifying the means by which to fight what at first seemed to be inchoate enemies such as al-Qaeda. That difficulty was 'solved' by waging war upon its host state, Afghanistan. The later advent of ISIS (Islamic State of Iraq and Syria) was almost a Godsend when it declared a caliphate upon its conquered territories. It meant a governing entity and a territory, a location, upon which massed state power could be plainly and visibly exercised. The Palestinian Authority, while not a fully-fledged state, has enough state-like characteristics to feel hegemony exercised over it.

Even so, actual non-state entities conferred simultaneous advantages and difficulties. One was the creation of the prison at Guantanamo Bay to house captured jihadi fighters from the war on Afghanistan onwards. It was a difficulty in that due process and the right to face trial were never granted the captives, and this created unease among advocates of human rights under law. But the laws of war are applicable only upon state actors and those representing and fighting for states. It was an advantage in that continuous imprisonment without due process represented a seemingly interminable warning to all non-state enemies of the American state.

The hegemonic state historically develops a panoply of state visibilities and public rituals; ceremonies invoking the clear receipt of blessings, the right to be blessed, and the right to impose itself upon others clearly less blessed. The state is declared righteous in the eyes of God. Erin Wilson has studied the State of the Union speeches by successive US presidents. They all conclude with the ringing invocation, almost an injunction to God, 'God bless America'. God exists as a relational figure to the American state, and the ritualistic end to the speeches simply expresses an assumption. Not 'man created in the image of God' but, rather, God created in the image of the state.[8] None of this is, as she points out, 'rational' in the sense of following an objective and secular logic. It is to do both with faith and its relationship to a political object of fidelity. Belief and patriotism become conflated. Karen Armstrong argues that the 'death of the spirit', both because of the vicissitudes of modern life – including wars and genocides – not to mention secular scepticism as an aftermath of the Enlightenment, means faith requires a material object to which spiritual imagery is appended.[9] She argues that this has been going on since the early prophets of Israel, but my argument here is that the creation of modern states gives this imagery a stronger and denser power because the state itself is more powerful than its pre-Westphalian ancestor. Faith validates power and state power elevates faith to a soteriological function in which the state represents the apotheosis of God's will. One is saved if God's state is saved.[10] These are of course powerful and sweeping statements but, at the very least, portray religion in its rhetorical function – with apocalypse being the antinomy of salvation. Millennials who preach and prophesy fire-laden doom, as well as salvation for the chosen, dramatically express the more mundane assumption that the state offers protection, salvation, justification and validation of often extreme practices – the alternative being too horrible to imagine.

So that, in today's triumphant but beleaguered Israel, the alternative to the Jewish state is simply annihilation, if not again of a people, of a personality in modern terms for a people – that is, as citizens of their own recognised state. And those people have to be the majority centrepiece of the state, a 'homeland for the Jews'. Others present cannot be regarded as members of the state, of the homeland.

And they cannot become a threat to not only the officialised members of the state but also to their political hegemony. Here, numbers of people and power become conflated. The Israeli scholar, Uriel Abulof, writes of an 'existential dread' that, one day, Palestinians, simply by faster breeding, will outnumber Jews – and the 'homeland for the Jews' will no longer be numerically the case. It will be a homeland for a more numerous 'other'.[11] In fact, it will take a lot of demographic escalation for this to occur, but that is why the Palestinian 'right to return' is such a controversial and difficult issue. An influx of returnees could overturn the population balance swiftly – thus there remains no 'right to return'. In the meantime, the denial of political rights to most Palestinians in Israel means that the Jewish population remains both more numerous and more politically powerful – a hegemonic population. If this population also occupies most of the land, economic hegemony seals the equation to the Jewish advantage. Those without rights become, as some would say is prophesied in the scriptures, 'hewers of wood and drawers of water' for the officialised possessors of the state, its land and its blessings.

The sense of just habitation – deliverance from the Holocaust, much like the first Passover angel relieving the chosen people from death so they could transit from Egypt, the 'House of Slavery' to the Promised Land, is not only a scriptural antecedent, but works alongside the immense and complex psychological relief of being saved from modern extermination. This complex condition is passed on to the succeeding generation. Using the words of the young US presidential inauguration poet, Amanda Gorman,

> Marianne Hirsch posits that the children of Holocaust
> Survivors grow up with memories of their parents' trauma[12]

Above all it justifies and casts all who are outside this justified frame as somehow associated with those who caused memory and postmemory to take their shape. These must be clearly marked as 'other', different and excludable.

The excludable are those already denigrated by God. In South Africa, one of the apartheid-justifying Lutheran tropes was the claim (not at all supported by scripture) that black people were the descendants of Ham, the son who dishonoured Noah after the flood and was cursed along with his offspring. Being discriminated against was simply an expression of that continuing curse. Similarly, in the United States, 'democracy' was in fact a very slow developer. Its history can be seen either as a slow, gradual but relentless inclusion, or a controlled protraction of exclusion.

The year 1825 saw President Andrew Jackson's democracy consisting only in suffrage for white adult males. Even here, a small number of residual property requirements remained in place until 1850 and, in fact, did not completely disappear until 1966. Black men had to wait until 1870, after the end of the Civil War. All women had to wait for national democratic rights until 1920, and Native Americans until 1924. Democracy was gendered and racist, grudgingly extended to those who had more 'naturally' served white men. And a panoply of scripture was used to 'prove' the inequality of women, the trope of Ham's descendants was wheeled out, and Native Americans, in any case, had been defeated. The nature of democratic advance was one that dealt slowly with categories of inferiority.[13] In Weber's Protestantism, hard work brought God-sanctioned prosperity and power over all those deemed to not have the same assiduous and voluntary work ethic that led to national hegemony.

In both the United States and Israel, all this is cast as an unchanging idea, a perpetual truth and an originating one. This truth is evident from scripture. Divinely animated antecedent, particularly in the Torah – the first five books of the Old Testament, those ascribed to the authorship of Moses, the one who was God's instrument in leading deliverance, the Exodus – is echoed in deliverance from the Holocaust, and continuing deliverance from those who would seek to usurp or diminish the State of Israel. And, even if the Torah was in fact the work of Ezra and his priestly reconstruction of history, that was itself in the aftermath of deliverance from Babylonian captivity. The image of deliverance is echoed in a string of replica ascriptions of God's hand at work: from Bob Marley's Rastafarian 'Exodus', to the Māori warrior prophets who made a syncretic religion drawn, in part, from Christianity to resist white settler colonialism,[14] to the United States needing to settle an untamed wild land and then resisting the power of the British Empire and, in latter days, the power of the vast communist challenge.

Nowhere is the hand of God and the justification by God more evident than in the fighting (and winning) of just wars. The Six Day War by Israel against Egypt was preemptive and born, in Michael Walzer's account, of fear and anticipation[15] – of dread in case Egypt struck first (although Egypt probably had no such intention). Walzer argues that the preemption was justified as Israel felt it could not depend on the Western powers to keep Egypt in check. But fighting alone and preemptively meant also a moral conviction that to do so was right: not just fear and dread but a sense of righteousness. Although it became a prodigious feat of arms and was victorious, the 'peace' (and occupation) afterwards was perhaps epitomised by Sydney Bailey's account of the (brief) planting of the Israeli flag over the Dome of the Rock in the Old City of Jerusalem and, for a longer time, over the Tomb of Abraham in Hebron.[16] The feat of arms had allowed rightful ownership of holy places, and the flag of the state represented a rightful alliance with holiness.

This echoes the sense portrayed by the US Library of Congress depiction of the American revolution:

Religion played a major role in the American Revolution by offering a moral sanction for opposition to the British – an assurance to the average American that revolution was justified in the sight of God. As a recent scholar has observed, 'by turning colonial resistance into a righteous cause, and by crying the message to all ranks in all parts of the colonies, ministers did the work of secular radicalism and did it better'.

The Revolution split some denominations, notably the Church of England, whose ministers were bound by oath to support the King, and the Quakers, who were traditionally pacifists.

The Revolution strengthened millennialist strains in American theology. At the beginning of the war some ministers were persuaded that, with God's help, America might become 'the principal Seat of the glorious Kingdom which Christ shall erect upon Earth in the latter Days'. Victory over the British was taken as a sign of God's partiality for America and stimulated an outpouring of millennialist expectations – the conviction that Christ would rule on earth for 1,000 years. This attitude combined with a groundswell of secular optimism about the future of America to create the buoyant mood of the new nation that became so evident after Jefferson assumed the presidency in 1801.[17]

The element of the location of God's 'Kingdom' on earth allows an ultimate patriotism. One is fighting not only for one's country, right or wrong, but fighting for God's kingdom, God's purpose, and, therefore, it cannot be wrong. Exodus from holocaust adds to the sense of divine salvation and divine purpose.

The Postscript of Possibilities

Undertaking a book on the religions of the Book, each of them with commonalities in terms of declared ancestries traced back to Abraham, but all of them with ancestral hatreds against the others not yet fully disappeared, even if restated and, to an extent, moderated in the discourse and strategies of modern interstate politics – together with accounts of how some religious conflicts are not at all moderated and their foundations reinforced – would not be complete without a statement as to how the nationalist and religious values of them all could be made to cohere in the quest for a more peaceful world.

This is not an attempt to stage a preposterous intervention. There is, for instance, no easy roadmap for peace between Israel and Palestine, no easy ecumenicalism that would satisfy Islamic and Christian fundamentalists. This chapter is also not a memorandum to the secretary-general of the United Nations. The aim here is, rather, to say something about reducing the literalisms in religions, to disembowel to some extent the embodiments of God as nationalist projects. This, in itself, is ambitious enough.

A word first on commonalities: in the Old Testament account, God promised to make the two sons of Abraham into mighty nations.[1] This has always been interpreted as the Jewish and the Arabic peoples. He did not say a word about perpetual war between them. That we may safely leave to the realm of politics – albeit with sizeable religious trimmings and not so sizeable fig leaves. Secondly, there has been a long history of Islamic commentaries on the works and words of Jesus – almost without exception to one extent or another favourable.[2] Taymiyyah, the purported inspiration and forebear of Wahhab, wrote such a work.[3] Thirdly, all three religions of the Book borrow from the same sources. Each is, according to Vilho Harle, a mirror image of the other.

101

The founder of Islam, prophet Muhammad saw himself as the successor to the tradition originated and represented earlier by the Israelites, the Jews and the Christians. Muhammad taught that earlier prophets had revealed the word of God to Jews and Christians; now to the Arabs, who had earlier remained outside the revelation, (who) had a prophet of their own in Muhammad. Whatever connections there are between the theological doctrines of Judaism, Christianity and Islam, it is clear that Muhammad adopted the doctrine of the distinction between good and evil, between God and Satan, from Judaism and Christianity, as well as from Zoroastrianism. Islam destroyed and replaced Zoroastrianism as a religion but simultaneously adopted many elements from it.[4]

As did Christianity, as noted in previous chapters. The connotation of darkness with Satan or a Satanic figure is key here. It allows a personalisation of darkness. Elaine Pagels observes that, in the Old Testament, Satan is merely a nuisance and an obstruction. I have observed how the Satanic creature flaunts himself in a goading way before God in the Book of Job. In the New Testament, he graduates to the status of Prince of Evil. The Gospels, written after the fall of Jerusalem at the hands of the Romans (although the Gospel of Mark may have been written a little earlier) speak to a schism between Jewish Christians and those Jews who refused the Gospels. Those who refused them saw Jewish Christians, like the Romans, as the enemies of God.[5] These writings were, therefore, part of a political divide over how to forward any Jewish project without a territory or capital city – the world, as a whole, that had deprived Jewishness of these things became an Other, a darkness, a dark kingdom. But, from the earliest book in the Old Testament and of the Torah, the test of humanity was always cast in this way: 'You must not eat of the tree of the knowledge of good and evil, for if you eat of it you will surely die'.[6] Bridging the gap, knowledge of how to bridge the gap, between light and dark would mean a solution to the mystery of the universe, and humanity was not ready for that.

Similarly in the conflicts between groups of Islamic believers, between Buddhists and Hindus, between Buddhists and Islamic believers, between communist parties and both Islamic and syncretic Chinese faiths, and in the reinforcement of foundations for conflict by today's Israel and United States, there is in every case something declared as an unbridgeable gap.

In the twenty-first century, it might at last be time to bridge that gap, to depersonalise evil as peoples and nations, to disembody good and evil, and see them as qualities and conditions not necessarily attached to Selves and Others, Satanic or otherwise.

This, however, goes against some four thousand years of history, in which notions, concepts and doctrines of God and godliness have developed – in remarkably similar ways – each developing, in part, by devising the sense of an enemy.[7] And each insisting upon the sanctity of its own body of belief. In the case of those with a Book, it becomes excluding and forbidding. Islam permits earlier Books, because the Prophet, when he came, fulfilled all that these earlier works pointed towards. It permits no later books. This would include the Book of Mormon, but that hardly intrudes upon the Middle East. It certainly includes the Kitáb-i-Aqdas, the book of the Bahá'í – a seriously persecuted religion in Iran – not least because the Bahá'í prophet, Bahá'u'lláh, established it as late as 1863, so it has none of Islam's venerability and, even though Bahá'í is accommodating of all faiths, the Kitáb-i-Aqdas is subtitled *The Most Holy Book*. The subtitle is taken as a challenge. It is a curious book, committed to ritual but reminiscent of Zoroastrian works. In some ways, it is a second coming of elements at least of Zoroastrianism and could easily be accommodated in any genealogy of books that does not insist upon privilege. But, outside Bahá'í, in the arguments of Judaism, Christianity and Islam, this points to a need to establish commonalities not just across faiths but also anchored in the Three Books and in faiths without Books – so that no one faith is postured as superior to the others.

Approaches to achieving this differ in fruitfulness and complexity – the most fruitful being the most complex. The easiest approach is to look for literal comparability, for example, reciting verses from the Books, the Vedic scriptures, the Buddhist scriptures that point to a common ethic – a basic exegesis that only leaves us with the question: 'Why do they continue to fight?' This last question was not attempted by Hans Kung, when he sought common ethics that were commonly applicable. But the step of application, and the test of commonality of application, is more difficult than the simple identification of similar verses. Even so, the seeming intent of the verse and its application still leave us in the realm of the literal, and verses that instruct us to love, leave us with questions about the ingredients of love and love's contingencies. None of this give us insight into common spiritual values other than there being some sort of common God – at least in His origins. We turn here, therefore, to a tradition that is upheld in one way or another across all religions, and that is hermeneutics.

Hermeneutics is a difficult concept to grasp in Western philosophical discussion. In the West, it was a borrowing from theological work of the sort associated with, for example, Teilhard de Chardin and Thomas Merton. It regards the insight of a scripture or scriptural teaching which is illuminating rather than didactic. Grasping the insight, being illuminated rather than instructed by it in the first instance, is an inexplicable process granted as much by grace as by intuition trained by long meditation and contemplation. It is not 'scientific'. In its transition to philosophy, it proposes a path that cannot to be taken by logic and linguistic analysis and is neither inductive nor deductive. The great German philosopher, deeply associated with hermeneutics, Gadamer, once said that it makes philosophy akin to poetry.[8] He denied that science could answers all questions as to how to face the future. And he accepted Wittgenstein's final edict in his *Tractatus* that what could not be expressed in words – that is, within the bounds of linguistically expressible reason – should be passed over in silence.[9] But this does not mean there is a blank at the end of reason. As Janik and Toulmin have argued in their intellectual biography of Wittgenstein, the transcendental nature of, for example, Buddhist thought leads to a (silent) resolution of those things reason cannot render into words.[10] In theology, it is perhaps a leap of faith. In philosophy it is a leap in thought.[11] It is a methodology of transcendence. But this made Christianity difficult for Gadamer. Here you have a religion that teaches things of the spirit; there is even a Holy Spirit; but then it all founders on the tension of Christ being made into a man, flesh is given to the Word and transcendence can be passed over by a retreat into the holy image of literalism.[12]

The French hermeneutician, Paul Ricoeur, elided the tensions between philosophy and theology by simply publishing throughout his life two separate voluminous bodies of work – one on each. But this was, in many ways, a pose. For instance, in his scientific works on Freud, one is drawn immediately into Freud's psychic drives that are not empirically verifiable, even if circumstantially compelling. The lack, however, of direct materiality in a drive, in an unconscious, immediately begins to propose a question to science. It also makes understanding of, for example, 'irrational' terrorism a series of not fully material propositions.[13] Ricoeur finally rendered his ideas into a sociability – that is, we congregate in a society of empathy whereby we are able to see ourselves as another; we share our thoughts and intuitions but are only able to recognise them in the tangibility of physical association.[14] We are not the hermits of solitude like Merton. In the recollections of his later years, Ricoeur also basically confessed that his works on philosophy and theology had, in any case, a common foundation in thought.[15] But, for Ricoeur, unlike Gadamer, the body was not a problem. The body of Christ was transactionable as a conduit to faith. But grace meant you could not stop at the body.

A French philosopher with Jewish ancestry, Emmanuel Levinas, wrote elegantly about the need for hermeneutics. He related the observation that the Talmud was written in the language of men. But this proposes a difficulty. God does not 'think' in the language of men. It is – in my terms, not those of Levinas – unlikely that He would be a grammar fascist. But this suggests that the language of men cannot capture the thought of God. Thus, there is a need for constant interpretation – even to return to the interpretation of the interpretation. There is a constant need for hermeneutics.

Because the strict contours of the verses outlined in the Holy Scriptures have a plain meaning which is also enigmatic. A hermeneutics is invited whose task is to extricate, from within the meaning immediately offered by the proposition, those meanings that are only implied. Do not these extricated meanings

have enigmas themselves? According to other methods, they in their turn must
be interpreted. And in the search for new teachings, hermeneutics incessantly
returns even to those verses which, though already interpreted, are inexhaust-
ible. A reading of Scripture, therefore, which is forever beginning again: a
revelation which is forever continued.[16]

It is a constant process of creation and recreation. In this process, even the
person and personality of God is constantly interrogated if not recreated. But
for Levinas, there is not a problem of God made flesh, as it was for Gadamer,
though not so much for Ricoeur. He writes that, in the Talmud, 'there is
an inseparable bond between God's descent and his elevation'.[17] For these
represent both God's power and His humility. Without these dual but contradictory attributes, there is no God in the Judaic and Christian formulations
and accounts. It is His humility which gives Him His power in a language
of cognisance among men. God is, to borrow language not used by Levinas,
in a constant state of dialectical relationship within Himself and able to be
appreciated dialectically by men. This, however, renders the idea of a static
infallibility untenable – and the reading of scripture in terms of infallibility
highly partial and limited.

Even so, the sense of God's elevation proposes an aspirational condition
for humanity, and it is a condition not bound by literal darkness and light.

If this depicts a hermeneutics of the spirit – that is, one that recognises
and seeks to deal with spiritual qualities that cannot be anchored literally – it
does not mean that no effort has been made to render hermeneutics scientific.
Aref Nayed, a respected Islamic thinker and ecumenical figure who has several times visited the Vatican in the spirit of mutual understanding, and who
was one of the leaders of the Benghazi uprising against Ghaddafi, wrote his
Canadian PhD thesis on an 'operational hermeneutics', in which scientific
criteria are apportioned to the various stages of constructing hermeneutical
enquiry.[18] This is a mirror of some of the procedures in linguistic analysis that
are foundations to analytical philosophy. But this is to 'nativise' the antidote
precisely to the logic of analytical philosophy and its empirical bedrocks in
which speech and 'reality' become logically consonant. The antidote in fact
relies on the sweeping illuminations of poetry and metaphors of the poets
such as Rumi and Hafiz, of Yunus Emre and the Sufi poets. These are the
poets admired by the young, unrigidified Khomeini, and which provided
Shari'ati with his means to develop (or re-develop) an illuminated Shi'a. In
the work of the doyen of both historical and modern Turkish culture, Talât
Halman, this is not simply a matter of the poets but of the Qur'an itself:

Islamic languages share the same word for poetry – *shi'r* – which is pronounced
somewhat like *sheer* poetry, and is. Poetry represents the best achievement of
of Islamic civilization/ the Koran is a wellspring of that achievement. Parts of it

might sound pedestrian in translation, but all of it provides a heightened poetic experience in the original Arabic. The word Koran means recitation – the chanting of God's wisdom in eloquence.[19]

Halman recognises, as indeed did Muhammad, that poetry is the language of rebellion. But it is also the language of God. In the search for meaning and interpretation of language, God fundamentally becomes a dialectical being and sponsor of dialectical thought. He escapes the question of the 'Grand Opponent', Satan, by opposing Himself.

Such statements can be made from the otherwise purely metaphysical meditations of both Hinduism and Buddhism.

It is idealistic to think that an approach to scriptures of this sort, to the books of the religions of the Book and those without a Book, or with many books, could become dominant, especially among religious leaders who are also embroiled in nationalist or internationalist projects. For them, scripture and God are instrumental, valedictory and telic – against designated enemies. Far from dialectical, God becomes an actor in a dyadic universe. This becomes a very literal, if not locally and geographically very small, universe in the contestation for land between Israel and Palestine. That land, from the view of *eretz* or biblical Israel, is bound by the borders achieved by Solomon – who, all the same, did not leave us any measurements of this land. He did leave us the second most puzzling book of the Old Testament, after the Book of Job, and that is the Song of Solomon.

There is no way to regard this book but as poetry and allegory, as metaphor. It is a book about sensuality, seduction and love's urgency. The king, who already has sixty wives and numberless virgins in line, is in love with a young black woman whose breasts have only recently fully developed. We assume she is, at minimum, sixteen. He is closer to sixty. They are in the passionate stage of love, pining and longing for each other. She searches the city for him and is sexually assaulted by the guards who pull her clothes away and beat her. We assume she is not raped. Her physical attributes are described in poetic detail, and she is, in modern feminist terms, thoroughly objectified. It is a deeply beautiful and thoroughly awful book.

But it is a book about longing, not unlike the longing for God in the work of Shari'ati. And, as a book of contrasts, love and brutality, it establishes a dialectic of love and its dramas and fears. She is a Shulamite, a dark woman, probably a Palestinian in today's terms. Her union with the Jewish king, a union celebrated by the daughters of an undivided Jerusalem, is a moment of joy. Here, the constant references to the carnality of two bodies represents both a unity and a disembodiment that reaches for a higher realm.

This is, yes, a somewhat idealistic way to finish – though not complete – this book. But, as I mentioned earlier, this book is not meant as a memorandum to the secretary-general of the United Nations. It is a written acknowledgement that there is more to the Books and books of religion than first meets the eye. Is it an epistle to religious leaders to rise above the literality, materialism and national parochiality of their teachings, their attempts to own God, or to own God for their nations or slices of nation. It is an epistle that asks them to preach of a God who is able to rise above the contradictions of Himself, become One with Himself, as the nations of the earth might become one in His – or Her – or, in today's search for pronouns, *Their*, luminosity.

A Problematic Afterword

The God of Blood

The 7 October 2023 Hamas attack on Israel left a bloody trail of death and destruction: some twelve hundred people were killed, 250 hostages were taken and there was much gratuitous violence and rape. The Israeli response, at time of writing (March 2024), in a volatile moment of Middle Eastern history has – by Israeli Defense Forces reckoning – killed one thousand of the original Hamas attack force of three thousand and, since then, twelve thousand additional Hamas fighters. Western observers consider Hamas a shattered force, although it has not been wiped out.[1]

That Israeli response has involved at least 186,000 flight hours, with aerial strikes against twenty-nine thousand targets in Gaza. Six thousand bombs were dropped in the first week of the Israeli offensive alone. About forty thousand Palestinian civilians in Gaza have been killed.[2] Universities, schools and hospitals have been attacked and vast swathes of Gaza flattened. What was described as a right to self-defence turned, it seemed, rapidly into revenge and then blood lust. In terms of numerical proportionality, almost forty times the number of deaths inflicted by Hamas on Israel have now been inflicted on Gaza. Much of the world's concern was expressed in the South African legal action against Israel at the International Court of Justice on 29 December 2023. The case was meticulously argued in legal language on both sides and, in my commentaries at the time, it seemed the South African arguments would carry the day.[3] As indeed they did, but to little effect; the war has continued and, using the Old Testament image of the force God used against Egypt to secure the release of the Israelites, God's Angel of Death has had a busy year.

The use of Old Testament imagery is purposeful. Much US support for Israel is predicated, as discussed in chapter 1 of this book, on the conviction of Jews being a chosen people with direct parallels to Americans also being the children of God. There is also the belief, trumpeted by Israeli politicians themselves, that the land of Israel belongs to the Jewish state alone, by historical right – although, as discussed earlier, that claim is at least arithmetically unsustainable.

But land is a centrepiece of the struggle between Israelis and Palestinians. The land occupied by both is extremely small. There is much struggle over very little. The two territories together are only 28,090 square kilometres – less than the land mass of Maine, Taiwan or Lesotho and marginally larger than Sicily; although none of these territories have two distinct nationalities contesting ownership of them.

Gaza itself is 365 square kilometres, smaller than Derry in Northern Ireland. Two million Gazans are crammed into it with little room for manoeuvre or exit.

Hamas is the government of this small territory, although it could claim to be the elected parliament of all Palestine. It won the Palestinian legislative elections in 2006, but war broke out between Hamas and Fatah, and Hamas was left only with Gaza. But even on the West Bank, controlled by Fatah, university students periodically vote in Hamas Student Representative Councils to protest the perceived nepotism and corruption of Fatah.[4]

As a radical organisation, linked in Egyptian governmental perceptions with the outlawed Muslim Brotherhood and with an original agenda that was plainly hostile to the existence of Israel, Hamas also made its early name by way of community service.[5] But it also expressed its hostility to Israel through attacks, including largely unguided rocket assaults. The Israeli response has been a series of invasions of Gaza, in addition to several more minor incursions. Major military assaults on Gaza took place in 2008, 2012, 2014 and 2021. Great damage and loss of life were caused on each of these occasions. The 2014 invasion was meant to destroy the Hamas tunnel network, through which militants could infiltrate Israel by travelling underneath the border. At the time, I wrote that the tunnel network was so sophisticated and complex that it could never be completely destroyed.[6] And indeed it wasn't. Israeli engineers in 2024 found the network even more sophisticated than before.[7]

The war in Gaza has attracted both Israeli support and opposition. Senior former military and other distinguished personnel have questioned its wisdom.[8] But Prime Minister Netanyahu has unstinting support from the Israeli right.[9] There is, in some quarters, a visceral hatred of Palestinian aspirations of any sort, Hamas being the tip of an iceberg of antipathy. In my own visits to Israel and Palestine, I have had as many guns pointed at me in close quarters as any African war zone I have monitored – simply for asking the 'wrong' question as to where the borders of an Israeli settlement ended with Palestinian land beyond.

Is there a way forwards in terms of agreement between extremes of policy preferences? Even the most optimistic scenarios are merely hopeful and contingent.[10] There is, even in an optimistic scenario, a hearts and minds exercise that needs to be successfully conducted in Israel itself. I myself am doubtful this will take place or succeed.

At the heart of what needs to be done, and on which agreement is extremely difficult, is the matter of who owns what land. The Oslo Accords have failed. What was meant to be Category C land, held in trust by the Israelis with a view to handing it over to the Palestinians, is now studded with Israeli settlements and farms. Much Category B land, meant to be jointly administered by Israel and Palestine, is also the site of settlements. The settlements are most unlikely to be retrenched, let alone demolished.

I recall an evening with the Berkeley-PhD-educated mayor of Bir Zeit (itself on Category B land) – a less pleasant evening than one on an earlier visit when we listened to an opera recital by a Japanese soprano performing in his living room. But on the latter evening, he forlornly asked, 'What will they leave us, Stephen?' And I replied, 'Only a necklace of "free" cities, not joined up, and all the arable land will become Israeli'. The later Trump plan to 'settle' the Israel–Palestine problem produced maps of land ownership that were precisely the necklace I predicted.[11] But there were roads linking the bits of necklace. Palestine becomes a strung-out emirate with no strategic depth or economic viability. And the settlements remain; meaning that there is no inherent contiguity of Palestinian territory. Even travel over a short distance will encounter a settlement. Ironically, under the Trump plan, Gaza is linked to the necklace by means of a very long tunnel.

But who will govern Gaza? No one is suggesting Hamas – even a democratically elected Hamas. The insertion of Fatah as government means an imposition upon Gazans who are not sympathetic towards Fatah, and no one is suggesting Fatah should be subject to the test of 'national' elections. With 'peace' will not come democracy.

The land left to the Palestinians will be far too small for any return of the Palestinian diaspora – something the Israelis have, in any case, always opposed. And this land will unlikely be able to be wrought into an internationally recognised state, with the rights of a state – with sovereignty over its own land, free access to the outside world through an airport and a port which has free access to the open sea. Such things are currently denied the Palestinian Authority and to Gaza with its seacoast. Their lack means the diaspora, even if it had the right to return, could not.

The era of the wandering Jew of recent aeons past would be replaced by the era of the wandering Palestinian. Not only Gaza but all of Palestine will scarcely be embodied under a nationalism within a nation-state.

A tenuous settlement of the current conflict may be achieved before the publication of this book. But if not Hamas, something like Hamas will likely rise again. Samson brought down the temple of the Philistines. But the Philistines were not prevented from waging war against the biblical Israel in the years that followed.

The prospect at time of writing is of an endless cycle of blood. Levinas talked of a luminous Judaism[12] – a Judaism of a luminous God. Under wise leadership, this should still be possible. Leadership open to the hermeneutic openness this book has suggested. Instead, in this moment when Judaism is enmeshed with a political and militarised project, it may remain a God of blood.

Notes

PREFACE

1. Elon Gilad, 'Who Really Wrote the Book of Job?', *Haaretz*, 14 September 2016, https://www.haaretz.com/jewish/MAGAZINE-who-really-wrote-the-book-of-job-1.5434183.

2. Stephen Chan, *Spear to the West: Thought and Recruitment in Violent Jihadism* (London: Hurst, 2019), 110–13.

CHAPTER 1

1. Angelo Rappoport, *Ancient Israel*, vol. 1 (London: Senate, 1995), 60–69.

2. Although it should be noted this 'Satan' is not strictly the Satan of Christian doctrine, he is certainly a 'devil's advocate' and certainly challenges God with Job as the pawn in an infernal betting game. Satan and Job himself have continued to evolve in our appreciations. See Stephen J. Vicchio, *Job in the Medieval World – Image of the Biblical Job: A History 2* (Eugene, OR: Wipf & Stock, 2006); see also Gustavo Gutierrez, *On Job: God-Talk and the Suffering of the Innocent* (New York: Orbis, 1987); and J. Gerald Janzen, *Job: Interpretation* (Louisville, KY: Westminster John Knox, 1997). The fascination with Job and his suffering acknowledge that this is one of the most problematic books of the Bible.

3. Jack Goody, *The Interface Between the Written and the Oral* (Cambridge: Cambridge University Press, 1987); Graham Furniss, *Orality: The Power of the Spoken Word* (New York: Palgrave Macmillan, 2004).

4. Edward W. Said, *Freud and the Non-European* (London: Verso, 2003).

5. Angelo Rappoport, *Ancient Israel: Myths and* Legends, vol. 1 (London: Senate, 1995), xxvii.

6. Andrew George (trans.), *The Epic of Gilgamesh* (Harmondsworth: Penguin Classics, 2002).

7. Wilfred Thesiger, *The Marsh Arabs* (Harmondsworth: Penguin Classics, 2007; first published 1964).

8. Hannah Lucinda Smith, 'Sail Like an Egyptian: Reed Boat Sets Out to Prove Herodotus Right', *The Times*, 3 August 2019, https://www.thetimes.co.uk/article/sail-like-an-egyptian-reed-boat-sets-out-to-prove-herodotus-right-r08h7qsbq.

9. Exodus 2.

10. Acts 7.

11. The tiny band of three hundred warriors marshalled by Gideon to resist (and overcome) the hugely larger army of Midianites became a celebrated episode in early Israeli national legend – Judges 7.

12. See Richard Elliot Friedman, *The Exodus: How It Happened and Why It Matters* (New York: Harper, 2017).

13. Israel Antiquities Authority Official Channel, 'A Huge 9000-Year-Old Prehistoric Settlement Was Exposed near Jerusalem', posted 17 July 2019, YouTube video, https://www.youtube.com/watch?v=sHh-eIRmI_4.

14. Benjamin Moser, *Sontag: Her Life* (London: Allen Lane, 2019), 203.

15. Nikolai Gogol (trans. Peter Constantine), *Taras Bulba* (New York: Modern Library/Random House, 2004), 121–22.

16. Lawrence Durrell, *Balthazar* (London: Faber & Faber, 1958).

17. An interview with Professor Derek Penslar conducted by William Eichler, 'Theodor Herzl and the Trajectory of Zionism', *Open Democracy*, 1 December 2016, https://www.opendemocracy.net/en/north-africa-west-asia/theodor-herzl-and-trajectory-of-zionism/.

18. Hannah Arendt, *Eichmann in Jerusalem: A Report on the Banality of Evil* (New York: Viking, 1963).

19. 'Walter Rothschild and the Balfour Declaration', The Rothschild Archive, n.d., https://www.rothschildarchive.org/family/family_interests/walter_rothschild_and_the_balfour_declaration.

20. Fred Uhlman, *Reunion* (London: Vintage, 1997).

21. Slavko Goldstein (trans. Michael Gable), *1941: The Year That Keeps Returning* (New York: New York Review Books, 2013).

22. Primo Levi, *If This Is a Man/The Truce* (London: Abacus, 1991); Primo Levi, *Moments of Reprieve* (London: Abacus, 1986).

23. Primo Levi, *If Not Now, When?* (London: Abacus, 1987).

24. Yad Vashem, 'Voices from the Inferno', The World Holocaust Remembrance Center, https://www.yadvashem.org/yv/en/exhibitions/warsaw_ghetto_testimonies/index.asp?gclid=EAIaIQobChMIsI2hnKe76QIVa4BQBh2VtAoMEAAYASAAEg-KV4vD_BwE, accessed 17 May 2020.

25. For the detailed, step by step, account of all this – and of all the Arab–Israeli wars that followed, up to that of 1973, see Sydney D. Bailey, *Dour Arab-Israel Wars and the Peace Process* (Houndmills: Macmillan, 1990). The account of pre-independence violence is given on pages 2–19.

26. Bailey, *Dour Arab-Israel Wars and the Peace Process*, still gives the most detailed and dispassionate account up to 1973. A pro-Israeli account, which also argues that the British aided the Arab side but takes the narrative up to the 1982

invasion of Lebanon, is by Chaim Herzog, *The Arab-Israeli Wars: War and Peace in the Middle East* (London: Cassell, 1982). Also by a Jewish author, but giving a very different point of view to that of Herzog, is Avi Shlaim, *The Iron Wall: Israel and the Arab World* (Harmondsworth: Penguin, 2014).

27. Clausewitz was a Prussian general who understood why Napoleon was able, time and again, to defeat the Prussians. His book is required reading on almost every war college curriculum around the world and is given credit even by guerrilla commanders: Carl von Clausewitz, *On War* (Oxford: Oxford University Press, 2008; first published 1832).

28. Colin Shindler, *The Triumph of Military Zionism: Nationalism and the Origins of the Israeli Right* (London: I. B. Tauris, 2010). Colin Shindler, *The Rise of the Israeli Right* (Cambridge: Cambridge University Press, 2015).

29. Colin Shindler, *The Land Beyond Promise: Israel, Likud and the Zionist Dream* (London: I. B. Tauris, 2002). Colin Shindler, *Israel, Likud and the Zionist Dream: Power, Politics and Ideology from Begin to Netanyahu* (London: I. B. Tauris, 1995).

30. Avi Shlaim, *Israel and Palestine: Reappraisals, Revisions, Refutations* (London: Verso, 2010).

31. Rafael Behr, 'Israel and Palestine: Reappraisals, Revisions, Refutations by Avi Shlaim', *The Guardian*, 3 October 2010, https://www.theguardian.com/books/2010/oct/03/avi-shlaim-israel-palestine-reappraisals-revisions-refutations.

32. Daniel Gavron, *The Kibbutz: Awakening from Utopia* (Landham, MD: Rowman & Littlefield, 2000).

33. Colin Shindler, *Israel and the European Left: Between Solidarity and Delegitimisation* (New York: Continuum, 2012).

34. Petter Bauck and Mohammed Omer (eds.), The Oslo Accords: A Critical Assessment (Cairo: American University in Cairo Press, 2016).

35. Uriel Abulof, 'Deep Securitization and Israel's "Demographic Demon"', *International Political Sociology* 8, no. 4 (2014): 396–415.

36. Noah J. Efron, *Real Jews: Secular vs Ultra-Orthodox and the Struggle for Jewish Identity in Israel* (New York: Basic Books, 2003).

37. Tariq Ali, *Conversations with Edward Said* (Oxford: Seagull, 2006), 90–91.

38. Khaled Hroub, *Hamas: Political Thought and Practice* (Washington DC: Institute for Palestine Studies, 2000); Khaled Hroub, *Hamas: A Beginner's Guide* (London: Pluto, 2006).

39. For my views on the wisdom and purposes of those Israeli punishment invasions of Gaza, see Stephen Chan, 'Israel's Stated Aims in Gaza Make No Sense – and Cannot Secure a Just Future', *The Conversation*, 25 July 2014, https://theconversation.com/israels-stated-aims-in-gaza-make-no-sense-and-cannot-secure-a-just-future-29631; Stephen Chan, 'The Hamas Government in Gaza Has Always Been a Tragic Mess', *The Conversation*, 29 July 2014, https://theconversation.com/the-hamas-government-in-gaza-has-always-been-a-tragic-mess-29795.

40. See Robert Fisk, *The Great War for Civilisation: The Conquest of the Middle East* (New York: Knopf, 2006).

CHAPTER 2

1. Norman Ricklets, 'How Angels Found Their Wings', *History Today* 72, no. 12 (2022): https://www.historytoday.com/archive/history-matters/how-angels-found -their-wings; Janelle Peters, 'Creation, Angels and Gender in Paul, Philo and the Dead Sea Scrolls', *Open Theology*, 7, no. 1 (2021): 248–55.

2. Maurice Casey, An Aramaic Approach to Q: Sources for the Gospels of Matthew and Luke (Cambridge: Cambridge University Press, 2002).

3. L. Ron Hubbard, *Dianetics: The Modern Science of Mental Health* (Copenhagen: New Era, 2007).

4. See Erin K. Wilson, *After Secularism: Rethinking Religion in Global Politics* (Houndmills: Palgrave Macmillan, 2012), chapter 4; see also Robert N. Bellah, 'Civil Religion in America', *Daedalus* 96, no. 1 (1967): 1–21.

5. Mika Aaltola, *Sowing the Seeds of Sacred: Political Religion of Contemporary World Order and American Era* (Leiden: Brill, 2008); see also Andrew L. Whitehead and Samuel L. Perry, *Taking America Back for God* (New York: Oxford University Press, 2020).

6. Emmanuel Levinas, *Beyond the Verse: Talmudic Readings and Lectures* (London: Continuum, 2007); Emmanuel Levinas, *In the Time of the Nations* (London: Continuum, 2007).

7. Emmanuel Levinas, *Difficult Freedom: Essays on Judaism* (Baltimore, MD: Johns Hopkins University Press, 1997).

8. Emmanuel Levinas, *Alterity and Transcendence* (New York: Columbia University Press, 2000).

9. Bernard-Henri Levy, *The Genius of Judaism* (New York: Random House, 2017).

10. Franklin D. Lewis, *Rumi Past and Present, East and West: The Life, Teachings and Poetry of Jalal al-Din Rumi* (Oxford: Oneworld, 2000).

11. Paul Gifford, *African Christianity: Its Public Role* (London: Hurst, 1998).

12. Paul Gifford and Steve Brouwer, *Exporting the American Gospel: Global Christian Fundamentalism* (London: Routledge, 1996).

13. Pierre Teilhard de Chardin, *Science and Christ* (New York: Harper & Row, 1965).

14. Pierre Teilhard de Chardin, *The Phenomenon of Man* (New York: Harper, 2008; first published 1955).

15. Pierre Teilhard de Chardin, *The Divine Milieu* (New York: Harper, 2001; first published 1957).

16. Thomas Merton, *The Seven Storey Mountain* (New York: Harcourt, 1948).

17. D. T. Suzuki, *Essays in Zen Buddhism: First Series* (New York: Grove Press, 1927); D. T. Suzuki, *Essays in Zen Buddhism: Second Series* (New York: Samuel Weiser, 1933); D. T. Suzuki, *Essays in Zen Buddhism: Third Series* (York Beach: Samuel Weiser, 1934).

18. Suzuki published his translation of the Lankavatara Sutra from the original Sanskrit (London: Routledge Kegan Paul, 1932).

19. Arnold J. Toynbee, *The World and the West* (Oxford: Oxford University Press, 1953). But see particularly the detailed study of the Toynbee/Suzuki correspondence: Paul Becque, 'Tragedy and the Limits of Reason: Arnold J. Toynbee's Search for a

Middle Way', unpublished University of Kent PhD thesis, 2009. I was the examiner of this thesis.

20. D. T. Suzuki, *An Introduction to Zen Buddhism*, with foreword by C. G. Jung (London: Rider & Company, 1948).

21. Thomas Merton, *Mystics and Zen Masters* (New York: Farrar, Straus & Griroux, 1986).

22. Thomas Merton, *The Way of Chuang Tzu* (New York: New Directions, 1969).

23. Thomas Merton, *The Way of Chuang Tzu*, with an introduction by the Dalai Lama (New York: New Directions, 2010).

24. Tenzin Gyatso, 'Many Faiths, One Truth', *New York Times*, 24 May 2010, https://www.nytimes.com/2010/05/25/opinion/25gyatso.html; 'The Dalai Lama and Thomas Merton', The Thomas Merton enter at Bellarmine University, http://merton.org/DalaiLama/, accessed 25 May 2020.

25. Hans J. Morgenthau, *Politics Among Nations: The Struggle for Power and Peace* (New York: Knopf, 1960).

26. Reinhold Niebuhr, 'The War and American Churches', in John A. Vasquez, *Classics of International Relations* (Englewood Cliffs: Prentice-Hall, 1990), 27–30.

27. Reinhold Niebuhr, *Christian Realism and Political Problems* (New York: Scribner, 1953).

28. Reinhold Niebuhr, *Moral Man and Immoral Society: A Study of Ethics and Politics* (New York: Scribner, 1932).

29. Reinhold Niebuhr, *The Nature and Destiny of Men: A Christian Interpretation* (New York: Scribner, 1943).

30. Reinhold Niebuhr, *The Irony of American History* (New York: Scribner, 1952).

31. For an account of this within his overall activism, see Jeremy L. Sabella, *An American Conscience: The Reinhold Niebuhr Story* (Grand Rapids, MI: Eerdmans, 2017).

32. Richard Wightman, *Reinhold Niebuhr: A Biography* (New York: Harper & Row, 1985), 91.

33. Joel A. Brown, 'The Klan, White Christianity, and the Past and Present | a Response to Kelly J. Baker by Randall J. Stephens', *Religion & Culture*, 26 June 2017, https://voices.uchicago.edu/religionculture/2017/06/26/the-klan-white-christianity-and-the-past-and-present-a-response-to-kelly-j-baker-by-randall-j-stephens/.

34. Morris West, *The Clowns of God* (New York: Hodder & Stoughton, 1981).

35. Glyn Burgess (trans.), *The Song of Roland* (London: Penguin, 1990).

36. Peter Such and John Hodgkinson (trans.), *The Poem of My Cid* (Warminster: Aris & Phillips, 1987).

37. Stephen Chan, *Plural International Relations in a Divided World* (Cambridge: Polity, 2017), chapter 1.

38. Immanuel Kant, *To Perpetual Peace: A Philosophical Sketch* (Indianapolis, IN: Hackett, 2003).

39. For a disquisition on this, see Janna Thompson, *Justice and World Order: A Philosophical Inquiry* (London: Routledge, 1992).

40. Mervyn Frost, *Towards a Normative Theory of International Relations* (Cambridge: Cambridge University Press, 1986).

41. Bradford Littlejohn, *The Bible and the Religion of the Protestants*, Davenant Institute, https://davenantinstitute.org/bible-religion-protestants, accessed 11 April 2018.

42. Barbara Goodrich, *The 'Protestant/Calvinist Work Ethic'*, http://www.ucdenver.edu/faculty-staff/bgoodric/Pages/Protestant-Calvinist-Work-Ethic.aspx, accessed 27 May 2020.

43. Max Weber, *The Protestant Ethic and the Spirit of Capitalism* (Oxford: Oxford University Press, 2011). Although Weber in later life changed much of his earlier view: Randall Collins, 'Weber's Last Theory of Capitalism: A Systematization', *American Sociological Review* 45, no. 9 (1980): 925–42.

44. Benjamin Franklin, 'Advice to a Young Trader', Founders Online, National Archives, https://founders.archives.gov/documents/Franklin/01-03-02-0130, accessed 28 May 2020 (emphasis in the original).

45. Nicholas V. Leone III, 'The Talents Parable: Timeless Economic and Investment Principles', Institute for Faith, Work, & Economics, 29 June 2018, https://tifwe.org/resource/the-parable-of-the-talents/.

46. St Augustine of Hippo, *The City of God* (Harmondsworth: Penguin, 2003).

47. Rolf Hochuth, *The Deputy* (London: Methuen, 1963).

48. Hannah Arendt, *Responsibility and Judgment* (New York: Schocken 2003) – contains Arendt's 1964 essays, 'The Deputy: Guilt by Silence?' and 'Personal Responsibility Under Dictatorship'.

49. John Cornwall, *Hitler's Pope: The Secret History of Pius XII* (New York: Viking, 1999).

50. John S. Conway, 'The Silence of Pope Pius XII', *The Review of Politics* 27, no. 1 (1965): 105–31.

51. Slavko Goldstein, *1941: The Year That Keeps Returning* (New York: New York Review Books, 2007).

52. B. C., 'What Happened to Liberation Theology?', *The Economist*, 5 November 2018, https://www.economist.com/the-economist-explains/2018/11/05/what-happened-to-liberation-theology.

53. Hans Kung and Helmut Schmidt (eds.), *A Global Ethic and Global Responsibilities: Two Declarations* (London: SCM, 1998).

54. John V. Tolan, *Saint Francis and the Sultan: The Curious History of a Christian-Muslim Encounter* (Oxford: Oxford University Press, 2009).

55. Trent Pomplun, *Jesuit on the Roof of the World: Ippolito Desideri's Mission to Eighteenth Century Tibet* (Oxford: Oxford University Press, 2010).

56. Jeff Mirus, 'Jesuits in Eighteenth-Century Tibet', *Catholic Culture*, 14 December 2009, https://www.catholicculture.org/commentary/jesuits-in-18th-century-tibet/.

CHAPTER 3

1. T. E. Lawrence, *Seven Pillars of Wisdom: A Triumph* (London: Penguin, 1962), 152.

2. Christopher de Bellaigue, *The Islamic Enlightenment: The Modern Struggle Between Faith and Reason* (London: Bodley Head, 2017), chapter 2.

3. Elie Kedourie, 'The End of the Ottoman Empire', *Journal of Contemporary History* 3, no. 4 (1968): 19–28.

4. Talat S. Halman, *Rapture and Revolution: Essays on Turkish Literature* (Syracuse: Syracuse University Press, 2007), Parts I and III.

5. Erik J. Zurcher, *Turkey: A Modern History* (London: I. B. Tauris, 2004), Part I.

6. Albert Hourani, Philip S. Khoury and Mary C. Wilson (eds.), *The Modern Middle East* (Berkeley: University of California Press, 1993), Part I.

7. Zurcher, *Turkey*, Part II.

8. Gerald Butt, *The Arabs: Myth and Reality* (London: I. B. Tauris, 1997), chapters 1–4.

9. Ghassan Salame, '"Strong" and "Weak" States: A Qualified Return to the *Muqqadimah*', in Giacomo Luciani (ed.), *The Arab State* (London: Routledge, 1990), 29–64.

10. James P. Piscatori, *Islam in a World of Nation-States* (Cambridge: Cambridge University Press, 1986), 13.

11. Raymond William Baker, *Islam Without Fear: Egypt and the New Islamists* (Cambridge, MA: Harvard University Press, 2003).

12. P. J. Vatikiotis, *Islam and the State* (London: Routledge, 1987), chapters 4 and 5.

13. Nazih Ayubi, *Political Islam: Religion and Politics in the Arab World* (London: Routledge, 1991), chapter 6.

14. Hisham Sharabi (ed.), *Theory, Politics and the Arab World: Critical Responses* (New York: Routledge, 1990).

15. Katerina Dalacoura, *Islam, Liberalisn & Human Rights* (London: I. B. Tauris, 1998).

16. Khaled Hroub, 'Introduction', in Khaled Hroub (ed.), *Political Islam: Context versus Ideology* (London: SAQI and SOAS, 2010), 13.

17. Moshe Ma'oz and Ilan Pappé (eds.), *Middle Eastern Politics and Ideas: A History from Within* (London: I. B. Tauris, 1997). Abdulaziz A. Al-Sudairi, *A Vision of the Middle East: An Intellectual Biography of Albert Hourani* (London: I. B. Tauris, 1999).

18. Peter Mandaville, *Transnational Muslim Politics: Reimaging the Umma* (Abingdon, UK: Routledge, 2001).

19. Said K. Aburish, *Nasser: The Last Arab* (London: Duckworth, 2005).

20. Neil Faulkner, *Lawrence of Arabia's War: The Arabs, the British and the Remaking of the Middle East in WWI* (New Haven, CT: Yale University Press, 2016).

21. Michael D. Berdine, *Redrawing the Middle East: Sir Mark Sykes, Imperialism and the Sykes-Picot Agreement* (London: I. B. Tauris, 2018).

22. T. E. Lawrence, *Crusader Castles* (Oxford: Clarendon, 1988; originally published in 1936).

23. S. E. Finer, *The Man on Horseback: The Role of the Military in Politics* (Harmondsworth: Peregrine, 1976), 112–16.

24. David Roberts, *The Ba'th and the Creation of Modern Syria* (Abingdon, UK: Routledge, 2013).

25. Marion Farouk-Slugett and Peter Slugett, *Iraq since 1958: From Revolution to Dictatorship* (London: I. B. Tauris, 2001), 92–102, for the early years of the Ba'th in Iraq.

26. Hanna Batatu, 'Of the Diversity of Iraqis, the Incohesiveness of their Society, and their Progress in the Monarchic Period toward a Consolidated Political Structure', in Hourani, Houry and Wilson (eds.), *The Modern Middle East*, esp. 502–14.

27. Faridu'd-Din 'Attar (trans. P. W. Avery), *The Speech of the Birds* (Cambridge: Islamic Texts Society, 1998).

28. I have written extensively about this: Stephen Chan, *The End of Certainty: Towards a New Internationalism* (London: Zed, 2009).

29. Michael Axworthy, *Iran: Empire of the Mind: A History from Zoroaster to the Present Day* (Harmondsworth: Penguin, 2008).

30. Ferdowsi (trans. Reuben Levy), *Shahnameh: The Epic of the Kings* (Tehran: Yassavoli, 2001), 180–81.

31. Joobin Bekhrad, 'The Obscure Religion that Shaped the West', BBC, 6 April 2017, https://www.bbc.com/culture/article/20170406-this-obscure-religion-shaped-the-west; James Barr, 'The Question of Religious Influence: The Case of Zoroastrianism, Judaism and Christianity', *Journal of the American Academy of Religion* 53, no. 2 (1985): 201–35.

32. US secretary of state John Kerry did come to realise this. For his account of the negotiations he conducted with his Iranian counterpart, see John Kerry, *Every Day Is Extra* (New York: Simon & Schuster, 2018), chapter 18.

33. *Christopher De Bellaigue, Patriot of Persia: Muhammad Mossadegh and a Tragic Anglo-American Coup (New York: Harper, 2013).*

34. Office of the Historian, 'Document 328, Editorial Note', Foreign Relations of the United States, 1952–1954, Iran, 1951–1954, Foreign Service Institute, United States Department of State, https://history.state.gov/historicaldocuments/frus1951-54Iran/d328, accessed 5 June 2020.

35. Jon Gambrell, 'US Quietly Publishes Once-Expunged Papers on 1953 Iran Coup', Associated Press, 29 June 2017, https://apnews.com/5111167bcaf84892b01eea93eea4bc01/US-quietly-publishes-once-expunged-papers-on-1953-Iran-coup.

36. M. Maksimov, 'The National Front in Iran', 28 October 1949, RGASPI, f. 82, op. 2, d. 1220, II. 30–32, Wilson Centre Digital Archive, https://digitalarchive.wilsoncenter.org/document/119116, accessed 5 June 2020.

37. David Patrikarakos, *Nuclear Iran: The Birth of an Atomic State* (London: I. B. Tauris, 2012).

38. Roham Alvandi, *Nixon, Kissinger, and the Shah: The United States and Iran in the Cold War* (Oxford: Oxford University Press, 2014).

39. Arshin Adib-Moghaddam (ed.), *A Critical Introduction to Khomeini* (Cambridge: Cambridge University Press, 2014).

40. Ephraim Karsh (ed.), *The Iran-Iraq War: Impact and Implications* (New York: Palgrave Macmillan, 1989). One of the survivors of that war, an Iranian colonel, became my PhD student and his was an account to me of no quarter. It was the longest and most costly war in what was called 'Third World' history.

41. Charles Tripp, *A History of Iraq* (Cambridge: Cambridge University Press, 2007).

42. The extent of this is the stuff of speculation. For a judicious rendition, see Nikki R. Keddie, 'Iranian Revolutions in a Comparative Perspective', in Hourani, Khoury and Wilson (eds.), *The Modern Middle East*, 617–18.

43. Philip G. Philip, 'The Islamic Revolution in Iran: Its Impact on Foreign Policy', in Stephen Chan and Andrew J. Williams (eds.), *Renegade States: The Evolution of Revolutionary Foreign Policy* (Manchester: Manchester University Press, 1994), 120–21.

44. Asghar Schirazi, *The Constitution of Iran: Politics and the State in the Islamic Republic* (London: I. B. Tauris, 1997).

45. Annabelle Sreberny-Mohammadi and Ali Mohammadi, *Small Media, Big Revolution: Communication, Culture, and the Iranian Revolution* (Minneapolis: Minnesota University Press, 1994).

46. Michel Foucault, 'Iran: The Spirit of a World Without Spirit', in Michel Foucault (ed. Lawrence D. Kritzman), *Politics, Philosophy, Culture: Interviews and Other Writings 1977–1984* (New York: Routledge, 1988), 211–24.

47. Ali Rahnema, *An Islamic Utopian: A Political Biography of Ali Shari'ati* (London: I. B. Tauris, 2000).

48. For example, 'A Brief Biography of Dr. Ali Shariati', Shariati.com, http://www.shariati.com/bio.html, accessed 7 June 2020.

49. Junaid Ahmad, 'Ali Shari'ati', *Oxford Bibliographies*, 24 April 2012, https://www.oxfordbibliographies.com/view/document/obo-9780195390155/obo-9780195390155-0141.xml, accessed 7 June 2020.

50. Jean-Paul Sartre, *Literary and Philosophical Essays* (London: Hutchinson, 1955), chapter 13.

51. Jean-Paul Sartre, *Existentialism and Humanism* (London: Methuen, 1948).

52. For an extensive study of Rumi's work and technique, see Franklin D. Lewis, *Rumi – Past and Present, East and West: The Life, Teachings and Poetry of Jalal al-Din Rumi* (Oxford: Oneworld, 2000).

53. I have here offered a very personal reading of Shari'ati. I have sought to write more fully about his thought in Stephen Chan, *Plural International Relations in a Divided World* (Cambridge: Polity, 2017), 100–105. Stephen Chan, *The End of Certainty: Towards a New Internationalism* (London: Zed, 2009), 225–35.

54. Henry Kissinger, *World Order: Reflections on the Character of Nations and the Course of History* (London: Allen Lane, 2014), chapter 3, esp. 134–41.

55. See Alexei Vassiliev, *The History of Saudi Arabia* (London: Saqi, 2013).

56. For an account of Wahhab's historical context and its contemporary echoes, see 'Abd Allāh al-Ṣāliḥ 'Uthaymīn, Dārat al-Malik 'Abd al-'Azīz, *Muhammad ibn 'Abd al-Wahhab: The Man and His Works* (London: I. B. Tauris, 2009).

57. Jonathan A. C. Brown, *Misquoting Muhammad: The Challenge and Choices of Interpreting the Prophet's Legacy* (London: Oneworld, 2015).

58. See my account of Taymiyyah in Stephen Chan, *Spear to the West: Thought and Recruitment in Violent Jihadism* (London: Hurst, 2019), 110–13.

59. 'Mecca 1979: The Mosque Siege that Changed the Course of Saudi History', BBC, 26 December 2019, https://www.bbc.co.uk/news/stories-50852379; BBC News Hindi, 'Islam and 15 Days of Drama', posted 29 November 2018, YouTube video, https://www.youtube.com/watch?v=zYoMZ5lZdrA.

60. Yaroslav Trofimov, *The Siege of Mecca: The Forgotten Uprising in Islam's Holiest Shrine* (London: Penguin, 2007).

61. Muslim-Americans on C-Span, 'The Siege of Mecca | Yaroslav Trofimov', posted on 23 October 2018, YouTube video, https://www.youtube.com/watch?v=1hNjJY1OXmM.

62. The visitor king Msm, 'Musharraf Saved Kaaba from Terrorists in 1979', posted by 18 December 2019, YouTube video, https://www.youtube.com/watch?v=bSKi5c87jZg; Roshni Light, 'Did Musharraf Really Saved Kaaba in 1979', posted 19 December 2019, YouTube video, https://www.youtube.com/watch?v=9wCASvvJgP0.

63. Nina Shea, 'Teaching Hate, Inspiring Terrorism: Saudi Arabia's Educational Curriculum', Hudson Institute, 19 July 2017, https://www.hudson.org/research/13778-teaching-hate-inspiring-terrorism-saudi-arabia-s-educational-curriculum, testimony to the US Foreign Affairs Committee.

64. Bruce Riedel, *What We Won: America's Secret War in Afghanistan* (Washington DC: Brookings, 2014).

65. For how this agency works, see Hein G. Kiessling, *Faith, Unity, Discipline: The ISI of Pakistan* (London: Hurst, 2016).

66. Ahmed Rashid, *Taliban: Islam, Oil and the New Great Game in Central Asia* (London: I. B. Tauris, 2000), chapter 1.

67. News report. https://www.youtube.com/watch?v=X-4THYku9vI&list=PLPp1F7IFcKeAu5e6skc4UtAaGTDuIDfNY&index=39&t=0s 20 January 2015.

68. Tariq Ramadan, *Western Muslims and the Future of Islam* (New York: Oxford University Press, 2003).

69. Curiously, the human drama and tragedy of this was very well caught in a graphic novel: Joe Sacco, *The Fixer: A Story from Sarajevo* (London: Jonathan Cape, 2004).

70. Gojko Beric, *Letters to the Celestial Serbs* (Sarajevo: self-published, 2001).

71. Yusuf al-Qaradawi, *Fiqh az-Zakat: A Comparative Study: The Rules, Regulations and Philosophy of Zakat in the Light of the Qur'an and Sunna* (London: Dar Al Taqwa, 1999).

72. Faisal Devji, *Landscapes of the Jihad: Militancy, Morality, Modernity* (London: Hurst, 2017).

73. Yusuf al-Qaradawi, *Fiqh al-Jihad: Dirasah Muqaranah li-Ahkamih wa Falsafatih fi Daw' al-Qur'an* (Cairo: Maktabat Wahbah, 2009).

74. For example, Sherman Jackson, 'The Appeal of Yusuf al-Qaradawi's Interpretation of Jihad'; and Sheikh Rachid al-Ghannouchi, 'What Is New about Yusuf al-Qaradawi's Jihad?', both in Elisabeth Kendall and Ewan Stein (eds.), *Twenty-First Century Jihad: Law, Society and Military Action* (London: I. B. Tauris, 2015), 312–33 and 334–50, respectively.

75. See *Islam in Contemporary Turkey: The Contributions of Fethullah Gulen*, special issue of *The Muslim World* 95, no. 3 (2005).

76. For critical but historically founded views and judgements see Alaa Al-Din Arafat, *The Rise of Islamism in Egypt* (New York: Palgrave Macmillan, 2017); Alaa Al-Din Arafat, *Egypt in Crisis: The Fall of Islamism and Prospects for Democratization* (New York: Palgrave Macmillan, 2018).

CHAPTER 4

1. On the nature and craftsmanship of these bricks, see the work of my School of Oriental and African Studies (SOAS) colleague Trevor Marchand, who himself learned to make them and helped in the curation of great buildings in Mali: https://eprints.soas.ac.uk/4940/; Trevor H. J. Marchand, *The Masons of Djenné* (Bloomington: Indiana University Press, 2009).

2. Alida Jay Boye and John O. Hunwick, photographs by Joseph Hunwick, *The Hidden Treasures of Timbuktu: Rediscovering Africa's Literary Culture* (New York: Thames & Hudson; Oslo: University of Oslo, 2008).

3. As part of a huge policy surge to emphasise science and learning: M. Daud Al Husaini, 'The Contribution of Islamic Universities of Andalusia to Revival of the Western World', *Global Journal of Human-Social Science: History, Archaeology & Anthropology* 14, no. 5 (2014): 15–23.

4. Mohammed Hussain Ahmed, 'When King of England Sent His Daughter to Study in Muslim University of Cordoba', *The Siasat Daily*, 23 September 2021, https://www.siasat.com/when-king-of-england-sent-his-daughter-to-study-in-muslim-university-of-cordoba-2195897/, accessed 1 August 2022.

5. Charlie English, *The Book Smugglers of Timbuktu: The Quest for This Storied City and the Race to Save Its Treasures* (London: Collins, 2017).

6. Alexander Thurston, *Jihadists of North Africa and the Sahel* (Cambridge: Cambridge University Press, 2020), esp. chapter 3.

7. Jeremy Lind and Caitriona Dowd, 'Understanding Insurgent Margins in Kenya, Nigeria and Mali', *Rapid Response Briefing*, issue 10, Brighton: Institute of Development Studies, March 2015.

8. 'Mali: Enabling Dialogue with the Jihadist Coalition JNIM', International Crisis Group, 10 December 2021, https://www.crisisgroup.org/africa/sahel/mali/306-mali-enabling-dialogue-jihadist-coalition-jnim.

9. Stephen Chan, *Spear to the West: Thought and Recruitment in Violent Jihadism* (London: Hurst, 2019).

10. Ahmed Adan, 'Ex-al-Shabab Leader Appointed Somali Cabinet Minister', BBC News, 2 August 2022, https://www.bbc.com/news/live/world-africa-61887107?ns_mchannel=social&ns_source=twitter&ns_campaign=bbc_live&ns_linkname=62e927912ea3472fbde823ff%26Ex-al-Shabab%20leader%20appointed%20Somali%20cabinet%20minister%262022-08-02T14%3A26%3A31.460Z&ns_fee=0&pinned_post_locator=urn:asset:bf512dc0-f44a-43e9-9604-2993ed0f1a9a&pinned_post_asset_id=62e927912ea3472fbde823ff&pinned_post_type=share.

11. Far from a Hollywood fiction. The author had a military colleague in Somalia who witnessed the entire event.

12. Paolo Tripodi (foreword by Stephen Chan), *The Colonial Legacy in Somalia: Rome and Mogadishu: From Colonial Administration to Operation Restore Hope* (London: Palgrave Macmillan, 1999).

13. Muuse Yuusuf, *The Genesis of the Civil War in Somalia: The Impact of Foreign Military Intervention on the Conflict* (London: I. B. Tauris, 2021).

14. In the image, he is shown wading to the Mogadishu shore carrying a sack of food over his shoulders. He became best known as the founder of Médecins Sans Frontières, and later as a French minister of health.

15. Matt Eversmann and Dan Schilling, *The Battle of Mogadishu: Firsthand Accounts from the Men of Task Force Ranger* (Toronto: Presidio Press, 2007).

16. See esp. chapter 6 of Yuusuf, *The Genesis of the Civil War in Somalia*, for a considered history of the ICU through the Ethiopian invasion to the emergence of al-Shabaab.

17. Stig Jarle Hansen, *Al-Shabaab in Somalia: The History and Ideology of a Militant Islamist Group, 2005–2012* (London: Hurst, 2013).

18. 'Considering Political Engagement with Al-Shabaab in Somalia', International Crisis Group, 21 June 2022, https://www.crisisgroup.org/africa/horn-africa/somalia /309-considering-political-engagement-al-shabaab-somalia.

19. Yuusuf, *The Genesis of the Civil War in Somalia*, 155.

20. Although under the much-publicised success were several problems: Olukunle Ojeleye, *The Politics of Post- and War Demobilisation Reintegration in Nigeria* (Farnham: Ashgate, 2010).

21. See my public discussion with leading Nigerian female politician and presidential candidate, Oby Ezekwesili, IgboConference, 'From Biafra to North East – Prof. Stephen Chan in Conversation with Dr Oby Ezekwesili', posted on 14 June 2017, YouTube video, https://www.youtube.com/watch?v=scKxpypie7g&list=PLP p1F7IFcKeBFtJz4KBo_tuTPCGwW79bT&index=53.

22. Daniel Jordan Smith, 'Corruption Complaints, Inequality and Ethnic Grievances in Post-Biafra Nigeria', *Third World Quarterly* 35, no. 5 (2014): 787–802, esp. 798–99.

23. Author's discussion with a former special adviser to a Nigerian president – names, date and location of which all agreed not to disclose – extensive in its account of political intrigue and its ubiquity, despite the obvious costs and consequences.

24. Lind and Dowd, 'Understanding Insurgent Margins in Kenya, Nigeria and Mali'.

25. SOAS University of London, 'Keynote: Nigeria between the Past and the Future: Culture, Governance and Development, SOAS', posted on 1 August 2017, YouTube video, https://www.youtube.com/watch?v=ciV5Vi-3Adw&list=PLPp1F7 IFcKeBFtJz4KBo_tuTPCGwW79bT&index=54, lecture given on 20 July 2017.

26. Fr Atta Barkindo, *How Boko Haram Exploits History and Memory* (London: Africa Research Institute Counterpoints, 2016).

27. Stephen Chan, 'Why Can't Nigeria's President Defeat Boko Haram?', *The Conversation*, 7 October 2016, https://theconversation.com/why-cant-nigerias-president-defeat-boko-haram-66581.

28. Modupe Oshikoya, 'Exploring the Impact of Insurgencies on Gender-Based Violence and the Nigerian Armed Forces: The Boko Haram Case', PhD dissertation, University of Massachusetts at Boston, 2018; Modupe Oshikoya, *Military Gender-Based Violence in Nigeria: Civilian Abuse in Conflict Zones* (Edinburgh: Edinburgh University Press, forthcoming).

CHAPTER 5

1. See Marilyn M. Rhie and Robert Thurman, *Wisdom and Compassion in the Sacred Art of Tibet* (New York: Harry N. Abrams, 2000).

2. See Swati Parashar, *Women and Militant Wars* (London: Routledge, 2014).

3. Roshan de Silva Wijeyeratne, *Nation, Constitutionalism and Buddhism in Sri Lanka* (London: Routledge, 2014), esp. chapters 7 and 8.

4. Wijeyeratne, *Nation, Constitutionalism and Buddhism in Sri Lanka*, chapters 6 and 9.

5. Paul Moorcraft, *Total Destruction of the Tamil Tigers: The Rare Victory of Sri Lanka's Long War* (Barnsley: Pen & Sword, 2012).

6. Mark Canning held ambassadorial tenure in Rangoon 2006 to 2009 and Harare 2009 to 2011. Our discussion in Harare was on 10 August 2010.

7. Asia Sentinel, 'Aung San Suu Kyi Fans Racist Flames in Hungary', *Asia Sentinel*, 8 June 2019, https://www.asiasentinel.com/p/aung-san-suu-kyi-racist-flames-hungary.

8. Hannah Beech, 'Myanmar's Monks, Leaders of Past Protests, Are Divided Over the Coup', *New York Times*, 28 August 2021, https://www.nytimes.com/2021/08/28/world/asia/myanmar-monks-coup.html.

9. 'Wirathu: Myanmar Military Releases Firebrand Buddhist Monk', BBC, 6 September 2021, https://www.bbc.co.uk/news/world-asia-58471535.

10. Stephen Levine, *Becoming Kuan Yin: The Evolution of Compassion* (Denver, CO: Weisner, 2013).

11. Sam van Schaik, *Tibet. A History* (New Haven, CT: Yale University Press, 2013), 2009.

12. See, for example, Gregory Rohlf, *Building New China, Colonizing Kokonor* (Lanham, MD: Lexington, 2016).

13. See Stephen Chan, 'A New Triptych for International Relations in the Twenty-First Century: Beyond Waltz and Beyond Lacan's Antigone, with a Note on the Falun Gong of China', *Global Society* 17, no. 2 (2003): 187–208.

14. See David A. Palmer, *Qigong Fever: Body, Science and Utopia in China* (London: Hurst, 2007).

15. For key books by the founder, with photographs of him performing Qi Gong, see Li Hongzhi, *China Falun Gong* (Hong Kong: Falun Fo Fa, 1999); and Li Hongzhi, *Zhuan Falun* (Hong Kong: Falun Fo Fa, 1998).

16. See Danny Schechter, *Falun Gong's Challenge to China: Spiritual Practice or 'Evil Cult'?* (New York: Akashic, 2000).

CHAPTER 6

1. Timothy Brennan, *Places of Mind: A Life of Edward Said* (London: Bloomsbury, 2021), 209.

2. Emmanuel Goldsmith, *Modern Yiddish Culture: The Story of The Yiddish Language Movement* (New York: Fordham University Press, 1997).

3. Rabbi Marc C. Angel, *Foundations of Sephardic Spirituality: The Inner Life of Jews in the Ottoman Empire* (Woodstock, VT: Jewish Lights, 2009).

4. Hannah Arendt, *Eichmann in Jerusalem: A Report on the Banality of Evil* (London: Penguin, 2006).

5. *Defiance*, directed by Edward Zwick, starring Daniel Craig (2008). See also the novel about Jewish guerrilla groups: Primo Levi, *If Not Now, When?* (London: Abacus, 1987).

6. Samuel Goldman, *God's Country: Christian Zionism in America* (Philadelphia, PA: University of Pennsylvania Press, 2018).

7. For one attempt at a (critical) biography, see Anshell Pfeffer, *Bibi: The Turbulent Life and Times of Benjamin Netanyahu* (New York: Basic Books, 2018).

8. Erin K. Wilson, *After Secularism: Rethinking Religion in Global Politics* (New York: Palgrave, 2012).

9. Karen Armstrong, 'Faith and Modernity' (worldwisdom.com), 2005, http://www.worldwisdom.com/public/viewpdf/default.aspx?article-title=Faith_and_Modernity_by_Karen_Armstrong.pdf, accessed 24 December 2022.

10. Mika Aatola, *Sowing the Seeds of the Sacred: Political Religion in Contemporary World Order and American Era* (London: Routledge/Republic of Letters, 2008).

11. Uriel Abulof, *The Zionist Absurd: Israel's Politics of Fear, Freedom and Bad Faith* (Oxford: Oxford University Press, 2021).

12. Amanda Gorman, *Poems: Call Us What We Carry* (London: Penguin Random House, 2021), 75.

13. Stephen Chan, 'Electoral and Intellectual Exercises in Validation', *Democratic Theory* 2, no. 2 (2015): 8–21.

14. Judith Binney, *Redemption Songs: A Life of Te Kooti Arikirangi Te Turuki* (Auckland, AUS: Auckland University Press, 1995).

15. Michael Walzer, *Just and Unjust Wars: A Moral Argument with Historical Illustrations* (New York: Basic Books, 1992), 85.

16. Sydney D. Bailey, *Four Arab-Israeli Wars and the Peace Process* (New York: Macmillan, 1990), 243.

17. 'Religion and the Founding of the American Republic', Library of Congress, https://www.loc.gov/exhibits/religion/rel03.html, accessed 24 April 2022.

THE POSTSCRIPT OF POSSIBILITIES

1. Genesis 17:19–21.

2. Tarif Khalidi, *The Muslim Jesus: Sayings and Stories in Islamic Literature* (Cambridge, MA: Harvard University Press, 2013).

3. Ibn Taymiyyah, *A Letter about Jesus Christ the Word of God* (Dublin: Alreshah, 2018).

4. Vilho Harle, *The Enemy with a Thousand Faces: The Tradition of the Other in Western Political Thought and History* (Westport: Praeger, 2000), 75.

5. Elaine Pagels, *The Origin of Satan* (London: Allen Lane, 1996).

6. Genesis 2:17.

7. Karen Armstrong, *A History of God: From Abraham to the Present: the 4000-Year Quest for God* (London: Heinemann, 1993).

8. Stephen Chan, 'Encountering the Philosophy of Hans-Georg Gadamer', *Contemporary Review* 290 (2008): n.p.

9. Ludwig Wittgenstein, *Tracatus Logico-Philosophicus* (New York: Dover, 1999; originally published in 1922), proposition 7.

10. Allan Janik and Stephen Toulmin, *Wittgenstein's Vienna* (New York: Touchstone, 1973).

11. The tension in Wittgenstein's two bodies of thought, the essential faith that ends the *Tractatus*, and his later linguistic theories, has been the subject of fierce debate: Kai Nielsen and D. Z. Phillips, *Wittgensteinian Fideism?* (London: SCM, 2005).

12. 'Interview: Hans-Georg Gadamer. "Without poets there is no philosophy"', *Radical Philosophy* 69 (1995): 27–35, here 35.

13. For my lengthy article on Ricoeur, see Stephen Chan, 'A Problem for IR: How Shall We Narrate the Saga of the Bestial Man?', *Global Society* 17, no. 4 (2003): 385–413.

14. Paul Ricoeur, *Oneself as Another* (Chicago: University of Chicago Press, 1992).

15. Paul Ricoeur, *Critique & Conviction* (New York: Columbia University Press, 1998).

16. Emmanuel Levinas, *Beyond the Verse* (London: Continuum, 2007), xiii.

17. Emmanuel Levinas, *In the Time of the Nations* (London: Continuum, 2007), 102.

18. Aref Ali Nayed, *Operational Hermeneutics: Interpretation as the Engagement of Operational Artifacts* (Dubai: Kalam, 2011).

19. Talât Halman, *Rapture and Revolution: Essays on Turkish Literature* (Syracuse, NY: Syracuse University Press, 2007), 35.

A PROBLEMATIC AFTERWORD

1. Neri Zilber and Andrew England, 'Hamas Has Been Shattered. Now It Is Fighting to Survive', *Financial Times*, 13 March 2024.

2. Emanuel Fabian, 'IDF Says 12 000 Hamas Fighters Killed in Gaza War, Double the Terror Group's Claim', *The Times of Israel*, 16 March 2024.

3. SABC News, 'SA Genocide Case Against Israel: Prof. Stephen Chan Weighs In', posted 24 January 2024, YouTube video, https://www.youtube.com/watch?v=oneaOgzb2Uk; Newzroom Afrika, 'SA Could Win Genocide Case Against Israel – Chan', posted 22 January 2024, YouTube video, https://www.youtube.com/watch?v=62O-y2nV9fc; SABC News, 'SA-Israel Genocide Case | Discussion on ICJ Order', posted 26 January 2024, YouTube video, https://www.youtube.com/watch?v=LhVn-RgW2_Oc, represent some of my commentaries on South African television as the case unfolded across January 2024.

4. As related to me by my graduate students at Bir Zeit University when I was Konrad Adenauer Professor of Academic Excellence there in 2015.

5. For dispassionate accounts of its early years, see the books by my former student: Khaled Hroub, *Hamas: A Beginner's Guide* (London: Pluto, 2006); and the denser *Hamas: Political Thought and Practice* (Washington, DC: Institute for Palestine Studies, 2000).

6. 'The Hamas Government in Gaza Has Always Been a Tragic Mess', The Conversation,
29 July 2014, https://theconversation.com/the-hamas-government-in-gaza-has-always-been-a-tragic-mess-29795; 'Israel's Stated Aims in Gaza Make No Sense – and Cannot Secure a Just Future', *The Conversation*, 25 July 2014, https://theconversation.com/israels-stated-aims-in-gaza-make-no-sense-and-cannot-secure-a-just-future-29631.

7. Firstpost, 'How Did Hamas Build "High-Tech" Tunnels Below Gaza? | Vantage with Palki Sharma', posted 21 December 2023, YouTube video, https://www.youtube.com/watch?v=L2xqfNowEs0, accessed 16 March 2024.

8. There has been longstanding opposition. See Guy Ziv, *Netanyahu vs The Generals: The Battle for Israel's Future* (Cambridge: Cambridge University Press, 2024). More recently, over the 2023/2024 invasion of Gaza: 'Senior Generals, Former Officials Demand Netanyahu's Removal', *Middle East Monitor*, 27 January 2024, https://www.middleeastmonitor.com/20240127-senior-generals-former-officials-demand-netanyahu-removal/.

9. Nerl Zilber, 'The Extremists Driving Netanyahu's Approach to War with Hamas', *Financial Times*, 19 February 2024, https://www.ft.com/content/e468283a-04de-4f33-9f10-5eaf4b1dc657.

10. Yuval Noah Harari, 'Is There a Way Out of the Israeli-Palestinian Trap?' *Financial Times*, 15 March 2024.

11. Peter Beaumont, 'Trump's Middle East Peace Plan: Key Points at a Glance', *The Guardian*, 28 January 2020, https://www.theguardian.com/world/2020/jan/28/trumps-middle-east-peace-plan-key-points-at-a-glance.

12. Emmanuel Levinas, *Difficult Freedom: Essays on Judaism* (Baltimore, MD: Johns Hopkins University Press, 1990).

Index

About the Author

Stephen Chan was awarded the OBE (Officer of the Order of the British Empire) by Queen Elizabeth in 2010 – 'For services to Africa and Higher Education'; The same year he was awarded the International Studies Association accolade, Eminent Scholar in Global Development. He has also been awarded in 2022 the Presidential Insignia by the president of Zambia. Formerly a newspaper editor and literary publisher, and an international civil servant stationed in Africa, Chan has held positions – including deanships – at three British universities; he has served as the George Soros Chair at the Central European University and the Konrad Adenauer Chair of Academic Excellence at the elite Palestinian Bir Zeit University, among a string of other named and honorific appointments. He is Professor of World Politics at SOAS University of London, remains seconded to diplomatic engagements in Africa and the Middle East and heads the philanthropic Kwok Meil Wah Foundation. He has published thirty-six scholarly books, five volumes of poetry and three novels.